COMMON ERRORS IN ENGLISH LANGUAGE

By the same author

REVISION EXERCISES AND TEST PAPERS IN ENGLISH
Ordinary Level Standard

AN ANTHOLOGY OF BRITAIN AT WORK

COMMON ERRORS
IN
ENGLISH LANGUAGE

BY

S. R. GOLDING, M.A., PH.D.

Formerly Chief Examiner
in English Language (Ordinary Level)
to the Associated Examining Board

MACMILLAN

First Edition 1964
Reprinted 1965, 1967, 1973

Published by
MACMILLAN EDUCATION LTD
Basingstoke and London

The Macmillan Company of Australia Pty Ltd Melbourne
The Macmillan Company of Canada Ltd Toronto
St Martin's Press Inc New York

Companies and representatives
throughout the world

Printed in Great Britain by
Biddles Ltd Guildford Surrey

PREFACE

The author does not take the view that the merit of a piece of writing is proportionate to the extent that it is free from mechanical error; that imaginative content and the graces of English style, for example, are of minor importance in the scale of literary values. He is, however, of the opinion that the rules of language should be treated with the same deference as the rules of sport, and that disciplined writing should not be made subservient to uninhibited self-expression.

The main purpose of this book is to teach students — especially those in the C.S.E. — G.C.E. Ordinary level range — how to avoid the more common technical errors to which reference is so often made in examiners' reports and for which a heavy penalty is sometimes exacted. Here, the author has drawn upon his wide experience as a teacher and an examiner, and upon the hundreds of reports he has received from assistant examiners over the past decade. The book should also prove useful to the general student who, without any particular examination in mind, is striving to acquire a feeling for sentence structure and variation and to express himself in intelligible English with a reasonable degree of correctness.

Each section (or sub-section) of the book follows the same pattern: expository matter, illustrative examples, exercises. It was thought advisable in the first of the three to make the language simple and the purely factual matter as short as possible. Furthermore, it has been borne in mind that many of the pupils using this book will be at the beginning of their fourth-year course, and that — particularly for those who have little linguistic ability and are not attracted to academic study — instruction by example, more so than by precept, would probably yield better results. Over 100 sets of exercises have been provided, with a concluding section of 100 miscellaneous sentences for correction. Throughout, an effort has been made to avoid technical terms, though simple grammatical terms have been used freely where they have been considered necessary to make an explanation more precise. The teacher will find ample material in this book for a two-year course.

The errors dealt with must not be regarded as exhaustive*; whether this error or that error was included depended solely upon its seriousness and frequency. The claim is not made for this elementary manual that it can take the place of a complete guide to spelling or punctuation, or of a textbook on grammar, or of a treatise on style. A word of warning at this stage would not be out of place. A student may have mastered every detail in every section of this book, yet with little reward for his diligence. If he is to derive the maximum benefit from the knowledge he has gained from these pages, if his aim is to express himself with lucidity and accuracy, he must have constant practice and apply what he has learnt to his ordinary day-to-day writing. He must, too, cultivate the habit of writing correctly, not merely in the subject labelled "English" but in every other subject of the curriculum, and even in the personal letters he writes outside his school or college. Above all, he must supplement his study of the correct use of language by wide and discriminating reading.

I have to thank Mr. B. C. Lucia, B.Sc., Secretary to the Associated Examining Board, for permission to state on the title-page that I was formerly Chief Examiner in English Language (Ordinary level) to the Board.

S.R.G.

* The student will find a more comprehensive treatment of the subject in *Current English Usage: A Concise Dictionary* by F. T. Wood (Macmillan).

ACKNOWLEDGMENTS

I am indebted to the following for permission to use copyright material:

Messrs Hodder & Stoughton, Ltd, for the extract from *Night Watches* by W. W. Jacobs;

Messrs William Blackwood & Sons, Ltd, for the extract from *The Power House* by John Buchan;

The author and Messrs William Heinemann, Ltd, for the extract from *Angel Pavement* by J. B. Priestley;

The author and Messrs William Collins, Sons & Co., Ltd, for the extract from *Maddon's Rock* by Hammond Innes.

S.R.G.

CONTENTS

I

SPELLING

Most spelling mistakes are due to ignorance, but a very large number are the result of carelessness and confusion. You have probably learnt how to spell the most common words — almost unconsciously — by reading. There are so many variations, however, in the spelling of each one of our vowel and consonantal sounds, so many peculiarities and irregularities in English spelling, that a quick glance at unfamiliar words in print is not sufficient if you want to avoid making numerous mistakes. You must look at each new word closely and commit it to your visual memory, so that you can tell immediately you write the word down whether its spelling *looks* correct. You must go further. Master the pronunciation of the word by saying it aloud, and make sure that you understand its meaning and can use it effectively in a sentence. Above all, treat your dictionary as a friend and consult it when you are in doubt. There are very few students who will be able to do all the exercises in this book without the aid of a dictionary. No attempt is made here to give a complete list of rules for spelling, but the few that are set out below, and the exercises on them, should prove helpful to students.

1. Carelessness

Some candidates in examinations misspell words on the question paper, and others in their haste omit one or more letters in words of two or more syllables.

EXERCISE

The blank space in each of the following words indicates where one or more letters have been omitted. Write out these twelve words correctly.

establis – ment, scul – tor, electri – ty, compe – tion, sat – fying, pol – cal, predom – nance, i – dividual, ever – body, edu – tion, apol – gy, p – ysician.

2. Confusion

(*a*) Even the very simple words in the pairs below are sometimes confused:

were	of	as	to	their	quite
where	off	has	too	there	quiet

(*b*) Confusion often arises when the two words are sounded alike or are similar in sound or appearance:

course	waist	lose	eminent	born
coarse	waste	loose	imminent	borne
choose	loth	divers	accept	draft
chose	loathe	diverse	except	draught

See page 42, under *Homophones*.

EXERCISE

Compose sentences, one sentence for each word, to show that you understand the difference in meaning between the words in each of the pairs in (*b*).

3. *ei* and *ie*

(*a*) When the *ei* or *ie* is sounded like *ee* in *he*, write *ie* except before *c*:

achieve belief pier hygiene
conceive deceit ceiling receipt

(*b*) When the *ei* or *ie* is not sounded like *ee* in *he*, write ***ei***:

height leisure neighbour forfeit veil

EXERCISE

Complete the spelling of each of the following words by putting *ei* or *ie* in the blank space: (Some exceptions to the rules have been included in the exercise.)

perc – ve, misch – vous, s – ze, s – ve, retr – ve, w – rd, fr – ght, pleb – an, conc – t, caval – r, th – ve, bes – ge, for – gn, handkerch – f, sk – n, inv – gle, h – ress, consc – nce, h – fer, n – ce.

4. Doubling of Consonants

(*a*) A word of one syllable containing a single vowel and ending in a single consonant has this consonant doubled when *-ing* or *-ed* is added:

fit fitting fitted
plot plotting plotted

Compare the following:

dream dreaming dreamed
toil toiling toiled

(*b*) A word of more than one syllable ending in a single consonant and accented on the last syllable has the consonant doubled when *-ing* or *-ed* is added:

refér referring referred
occúr occurring occurred

Compare the following where the accent is *not* on the last syllable:

ballot	balloting	balloted
offer	offering	offered

(*c*) A word ending in *-l* generally doubles the *-l* when a suffix is added:

jewe*ll*er enro*ll*ed unriva*ll*ed quarre*ll*ing

EXERCISE

Write out the correct spellings of the following words when *-ing* and *-ed* are added: (Some exceptions to the rules have been included in the exercise.)

handicap, initial, banquet, groan, profit, submit, gambol, develop, worship, infer, level, sin, rivet, benefit, kidnap, horsewhip, marshal, murmur, debar, appeal.

5. Words Ending in a Consonant + *e*

(*a*) These words usually drop the *-e* when a suffix beginning with a vowel is added:

use	reverse	revise	forgive
usable	reversible	revising	forgivable

(*b*) In order to preserve the soft sound, the *-e* is often retained when it is preceded by *-c* or *-g*:

peace	manage	notice	change
peaceable	manageable	noticeable	changeable

EXERCISE

Write out the correct spellings of the following words when *-able* is added: (Some exceptions to the rules have been included in the exercise.)

move, note, trace, compare, solve, marriage, tame, debate, service, tune, excite, charge, adore, live, sale, like, rate, pronounce, desire, palate.

6. Vowel Suffixes

Students are often in doubt about the use of the following suffixes: *-ance* or *-ence*; *-able* or *-ible*; *-ous* or *-eous* or *-ious*; *-ary* or *-ery* or *-ory*.

EXERCISES

1. Add either *-ance* or *-ence* to each of the following words, making any change that is necessary in the spelling:

resist, exist, encumber, guide, superintend, precede, acquaint, adhere, condole, ally, brilliant, luxury, persevere, prefer, recur, depend, persist, abhor, remit, vigil.

2. Add in a similar way either *-able* or *-ible*:

pass, access, discern, regret, inflame, practice, divide, reduce, collapse, charity, gull, rely, value, sense, horrid, repress, vary, duty, force, accept.

3. Add in a similar way either *-ous* or *-eous* or *ious*:

circuit, gas, victor, poison, censor, office, instant, ceremony, merit, humour, disaster, contemporary, plenty, libel, pity, caprice, rebel, outrage, wonder, study.

4. Add in a similar way either *-ary* or *-ery* or *-ory*:

arbiter, buffoon, advise, deposit, oblige, element, gloss, honour, cajole, distil, prepare, reform, image, legend, fool, conserve, stipend, refine, example, statute.

5. Add the suffix in brackets to each of the following words, making any change that is necessary in the spelling:

acquire (*-tion*), repertoire (*-ory*), brief (*-ity*), sage (*-ious*), metal (*-ic*), current (*-cy*), brag (*-art*), zigzag (*-ing*), curve (*-ure*), merchant (*-ile*), thrall (*-dom*), military (*-ism*).

observe (*-ory*), denounce (*-tion*), pompous (*-ity*), prevail (*-ent*), finance (*-er*), genteel (*-ity*), repair (*-tion*), likely

(*-hood*), epistle (*-ary*), authority (*-ive*), clique (*-ish*), expel-(*-sion*).

bivouac (*-ed*), curve (*-ure*), ellipse (*-al*), grain (*-ary*), instant (*-eous*), merry (*-ment*), propaganda (*-ist*), sly (*-ness*), influence (*-ial*), sympathy (*-ic*), spectacle (*-ar*), opaque (*-ity*).

7. Silent Letters

There are many words in the English language containing one or more letters which are not sounded: e.g. g*h*ost, *p*sa*l*mist, trunch*e*on, vic*tu*als, hau*gh*ty.

EXERCISE

Write down the letters that are not sounded in the following words:

catacomb, indict, schism, depot, mortgage, viscount, corps, raspberry, impugn, almond, knapsack, parliament, dahlia, furlough, poignant, rhapsody, halfpenny, solemn, rheumatism, circuit.

8. Difficult Words

Jot down in a note book all words that trouble you in spelling.

EXERCISES

1. Complete the following words by putting one or more vowels (including *y* when it is not used as a consonant) in each of the blank spaces. The 36 words are in alphabetical order.

e.g. – cc – d – nt – ll –, accidentally;
gl – c – r – n –, glycerine;
st – t – st – c – n, statistician.

– cc – l – r – t – n, – cc – mm – d – t – n, – dv – rt – s – m – nt, – v – rd – p – s, c – mp – r – t – v –, c – nsc – nt – s, c – nv – l – sc – nc –, d – s – cc – t – d, d – phr – gm, d – phth – r –, – nc – cl – p – d –, – v – p – r – t – n.

F – hr – nh – t, g – mkh – n –, h – m – rrh – g –, h – p – th – s – s, l – t – n – nt, l – q – f –, m – nt – lp – c –, m – th – m – t – c – n, m – t – r – l – g – c – l, m – sc – ll – n – s, p – r – ff – n, ph – n – m – n – n.

pn – m – t – c, pr – n – nc – t – n, pr – p – ll – r, ps – ch – l – g –, r – c – nn – tr –, rh – d – d – ndr – n, s – cch – r – n –, s – rg – nt, s – bt – rr – n – n, s – mm – tr –, t – b – gg – n, v – c – ss – t – d –.

2. The following passage has been taken from Holinshed's *Chronicles of Englande, Scotlande, and Irelande* (1577). Write down the present-day spelling of all the words in the passage that were spelt differently about 400 years ago.

> When he [Henry V] had thus ordered his battels, he left a small companie to keepe his campe and cariage, which remained still in the village, and then calling his capteins and soldiers about him, he made to them a right grave oration, mooving them to plaie the men, whereby to obteine a glorious victorie, as there was hope certaine they should, the rather if they would but remember the just cause for which they fought, and whome they should incounter, such faint-hearted people as their ancestors had so often overcome. To conclude, manie words of courage he uttered, to stirre them to doo manfullie, assuring them that England should never be charged with his ransome, nor anie Frenchman triumph over him as a captive.

II

STRUCTURE OF SENTENCES

Candidates are severely handicapped throughout the whole of the English Language paper if they do not fully understand the structure of the different kinds of sentences, and the distinction between a sentence on the one hand and a clause or a phrase on the other.

See the INDEX under each of the following: *Phrases*, *Clauses*, *Sentences*.

1. Phrases

A phrase* is a combination of words that has no predicate. Unlike a sentence or a clause, therefore, a phrase has no finite verb. One phrase in each of the following sentences has been put in italics:

Necessity is *the mother of invention.*
He felt very tired *after his day's work.*
Nearly overcome by the fumes, she shouted for help.

EXERCISE

Introduce each of the following phrases into a sentence:

in accordance with; on behalf of; for example; with regard to; in order to conceal her identity; against the wishes of; impatient with his nephew; releasing him from his promise; exhausted after her game of tennis; how to write an effective letter; to be acceptable; the difference between.

* Limited by some grammarians to a combination of words that contains no finite verb and does the work of a single part of speech: e.g. "A student *in our college* has been commended for his bravery." (adjective) "Empress Eugénie died in 1920 *at the age of ninety-four*." (adverb)

2. Clauses

A clause is a combination of words that has a predicate and is part of a larger sentence.

There are two clauses in each of the following sentences — a main clause, and a subordinate clause (in italics):

When I grew older, I ceased to wonder at the creature's presence.

Those on shore cried out to us *that they were not interested in our catch.*

The rider *who came first in the speedway race* was cheered loudly by the crowd.

EXERCISE

Make the following clauses into sentences by writing a clause in each of the blank spaces:

(*a*) That you have deceived me ....
(*b*) .... whom I recommend for the position.
(*c*) .... which was placed on my table.
(*d*) Should you decide otherwise, ...
(*e*) My view is ....
(*f*) As we have not yet settled our dispute, ...
(*g*) .... in order that you may be present at the meeting.
(*h*) .... when the incident occurred.
(*i*) How pleasant it is to recall the time ....
(*j*) .... who is the guilty person?

3. Sentences

A sentence is a combination of words that makes complete sense:

A thermostat is an automatic device for regulating temperature.

Assuaging his thirst from a nearby stream, the explorer felt sufficiently refreshed to travel onwards into the unknown territory that lay stretched out before him.

As I knew that this was a neighbourhood studded with great manors, I left Shalah by the fire with such food as remained and set out to look for human habitation.

EXERCISES

1. Define each of the following in one sentence:

a plate, a chisel, a button, a football, a sofa, a jersey, a spade, a canoe, a drum, a telescope.

2. Explain clearly, in one sentence for each, what you understand by the following:

a correspondence course; a hitch-hiking holiday; a barbacue; a jumble sale; a Brains Trust; a regatta; a supermarket; a youth hostel; a concert; a documentary film.

3. Describe, in one sentence for each, the work of the following:

a journalist; an auctioneer; a masseur; a sculptor; an oculist; a milliner; a pharmacist; an upholsterer; a solicitor; an almoner.

4. Write a sentence to describe the use of each of the following:

a pressure-cooker; a vacuum flask; a cine-camera; a dictaphone; a duplicator; a megaphone; a chronometer; a microscope; a barometer; a stethoscope.

5. The following words are connected with books and reading. Give an explanation of each in one sentence.

a diary; an album; a sequel; a bibliography; an anthology; an autograph; a manuscript; a classic; a magazine; a leaflet.

6. Define each of the following in one sentence:

astronomy, archaeology, etymology, botany, biology, psychology, geology, ethics, economics, zoology.

7. Define each of the following in one sentence:

emigration, pacifism, nationalisation, dictatorship, census, conscription, neutrality, propaganda, extradition, imperialism.

8. Write an answer *in one sentence* to each of the following questions:

(*a*) What are "the three Rs"?

(*b*) What is the difference in meaning between the following sentences: "This is the *latest* edition of *The Argus*" and "This is the *last* edition of *The Argus*"?

(*c*) What is the origin of the expression "a red-letter day"?

(*d*) What is the main difference between "an opera" and "a ballet"?

(*e*) What is wrong with the following sentence: "Furniture from the Middle Ages is hard to get, but if it is unobtainable it can always be made by your local carpenter"?

(*f*) What is "a dead language"?

(*g*) What is the meaning of the following proverb: "Those who live in glass houses should not throw stones"?

(*h*) What is "a co-educational school"?

(*i*) What does *secondary* mean when we speak about "secondary education"?

(*j*) What subject in your school curriculum do you like best, and why?

4. Combination of Sentences

A succession of sentences, with little variation in their structure, is boring to the reader. You should aim at a pleasing variety in your sentences and not rely solely upon the simple or compound type of sentence. Make sure, however, that your powers of craftsmanship are equal to the task of writing complex and complex-compound (multiple) sentences. The over-ambitious student, in seeking to avoid a series of short, jerky sentences, must guard against the danger of writing long and involved sentences that are loosely connected and weak in structure.

The following are some of the ways in which two or more sentences can be combined into *one* well-constructed and harmonious sentence:

(*a*) By the use of conjunctions:

My son came first in the mile race. He also came first in the high jump.

My son came first *both* in the mile race *and* in the high jump.

John works very hard indeed at school. He is most anxious to qualify for admission to a university.

John works very hard indeed at school *because* he is most anxious to qualify for admission to a university.

See pages 25–27.

(*b*) By the use of relative pronouns:

Shakespeare was born in 1564 and died in 1616. He is undoubtedly the greatest of all English writers.

Shakespeare, *who* is undoubtedly the greatest of all English writers, was born in 1564 and died in 1616.

I have made every effort to find the book. I borrowed it from a friend about a fortnight ago.

I have made every effort to find the book *which* I borrowed from a friend about a fortnight ago.

(*c*) By the use of participles:

He was bribed by the Spartans. The spy gave them a good deal of information about the Athenian army.

Having been bribed by the Spartans, the spy gave them a good deal of information about the Athenian army.

The police cleared the streets of the demonstrators. The housewives felt safe to leave their houses to do their morning shopping.

The police *having cleared* the streets of the demonstrators, the housewives felt safe to leave their houses to do their morning shopping.

(*d*) By the use of phrases in apposition:

George Manville Fenn wrote more than 170 books. He was educated at Battersea Training College.

George Manville Fenn, *the writer of more than* 170 *books*, was educated at Battersea Training College.

The Golden Gate Bridge is one of the world's greatest bridges. It is at the entrance to the Bay of San Francisco, California.

The Golden Gate Bridge, *one of the world's greatest bridges*, is at the entrance to the Bay of San Francisco, California.

(*e*) By the use of prepositions:

The damage to the apparatus must have been done by some of the club members. The gym instructor did not arrive until 7.10 p.m.

The damage to the apparatus must have been done by some of the club members *before* the arrival of the gym instructor at 7.10 p.m.

Hilda Johnson saved the baby's life. She rushed into the burning building and carried the baby out to safety.

Hilda Johnson saved the baby's life *by* rushing into the burning building and carrying the baby out to safety.

(*f*) By the use of infinitives:

Giles Haton asked the bank for a loan of £2,000. He is extending his business premises in Connaught Street.

Giles Haton asked the bank for a loan of £2,000 *to extend* his business premises in Connaught Street.

The actress attired herself in a multi-coloured costume and a black silk hat. She dressed up in this way with the object of making the children laugh.

The actress attired herself in a multi-coloured costume and a black silk hat in order *to make* the children laugh.

The following examples show how more than two sentences can be combined into one sentence:

Three sentences. James scored a century in his first trial match. He was given a place in St. Minster's Cricket XI. He did not come up to expectation, however, in the first two matches that were played against other schools.

One sentence. Having scored a century in his first trial match, James was given a place in St. Minster's Cricket XI; but he did not come up to expectation in the first two matches that were played against other schools.

Four sentences. Mr. Downham is chairman of the Sefton Cultural Society. The Society has been in existence for nearly 20 years. He left home at 4 o'clock to catch a train for Sefton. He was going to deliver a lecture to the students of the local college.

One sentence. Mr. Downham, chairman of the Sefton Cultural Society, which has been in existence for nearly 20 years, left home at 4 o'clock to catch a train for Sefton, where he was going to deliver a lecture to the students of the local college.

Five sentences. I am opposed to a General Election at the present time. I have strong views on this subject. A General Election now would rightly be regarded as an unfair advantage taken by the Party in power. A General Election now would also play into the hands of our opponents. Finally, a General Election now would not be in the best interests of the country.

One sentence. I am strongly opposed to a General Election at the present time for several reasons: a General Election now would rightly be regarded as an unfair advantage taken by the Party in power; it would play into the hands of our opponents; finally, it would not be in the best interests of the country.

EXERCISES

1. Combine each of the following pairs of sentences into one well-constructed sentence:

(*a*) In 1497 Sir Thomas More went to Oxford. There he became the friend of Erasmus.

(*b*) This is the first problem we have to solve. The problem is how to seat so many people in such a small hall.

(*c*) John watched the man striding away along the deserted road. He then mounted his cycle and once more headed south.

(*d*) He did not have to wait long at the hospital. The doctor examined his leg.

(*e*) My tailor has 100 winter coats in his shop. He must sell them by the end of this month.

(*f*) Covent Garden, in London, is now a great flower and fruit market. It was once a convent garden owned by the abbot and monks of Westminster.

(*g*) Jack's face was covered with grime from removing the soot. I did not recognise him.

(*h*) He speaks French fluently. He also has a wide knowledge of French literature.

(*i*) Our old house is now for sale. We spent many happy years there during our childhood.

(*j*) The harp is one of the most ancient of stringed

instruments. Its earliest forms seem to have been suggested by the hunting bow.

2. Combine each of the following groups of sentences into one well-constructed sentence:

(*a*) He did not buy the house for himself. He bought it for his son and daughter-in-law. They had a hard struggle to make a living.

(*b*) We crept upstairs. We were careful not to wake the other inmates of the house. Two of them were also escaped prisoners of war.

(*c*) Nothing could have been worse for the development of my mind than Dr. Pinton's school. Dr. Pinton was a classical scholar. He displayed very little interest in the sciences.

(*d*) The final assault on Harper's Ferry was entrusted to eighty United States marines. They had arrived during the night with two cannon. They were under the command of Colonel Robert Lee.

(*e*) The lion saw me running towards him. The lion took up his station under a tree. Here he was half hidden by some low bushes. Above these bushes only his head showed.

(*f*) Newton was a country boy. He was born on Christmas Day, 1642. He was born in a small stone-built farmhouse. The farmhouse stands near the village of Colsterworth in Lincolnshire.

(*g*) Gerald Williams left Oxford without taking a degree. His parents were very much annoyed with him. He decided to emigrate to New Zealand. He was of the opinion that there was no future for him in this country.

(*h*) An Oxford and Cambridge expedition has reached Roraima. It lies at the point where Venezuela, British Guiana and Brazil meet. It is cut off from the rest of the world by high cliffs. This mysterious mountain inspired Conan Doyle's book *The Lost World*.

(*i*) We walked about half a mile. We came upon a dry watercourse. There we observed the old foot-marks of a tapir. A little later, we observed the fresh tracks of a jaguar. We observed the fresh tracks of the jaguar on the margin of a curious circular hole full of muddy water.

(*j*) Arkwright was the inventor of the spinning-frame. It was an improvement on Hargreaves's spinning-jenny. Arkwright took out a patent for his machine in 1769. Arkwright was the founder in England of the modern factory system. This system has proved a source of immense wealth to individuals and to nations.

5. Excessive Use of *and* and *then*

A very common fault is the excessive use of these two words to link two or more clauses together. Too many ideas are usually packed into the one sentence. Note the improved version in the second of the two passages in each of the following pairs:

I thought I would provide a little entertainment for the native porters and so I stepped on to the footplate and then blew off the steam and at the same time I sounded the whistle.

With a view to providing a little entertainment for the native porters, I stepped on to the footplate and blew off the steam, at the same time as I sounded the whistle.

It was Sir Walter Scott's practice to rise at 5 o'clock and then light his own fire and he was usually seated at his desk by 6 o'clock and thus by the time the family assembled for breakfast at 10 o'clock he had already done four hours' work.

It was Sir Walter Scott's practice to rise at 5 o'clock and light his own fire. Thus, as he was usually seated at his desk by 6 o'clock, he had already done four hours' work by the time the family assembled for breakfast at 10 o'clock.

When I go to the library, the first thing I do is to hand in my book to the librarian and then afterwards I consult the card index and then I look for my book on the shelves.

When I go to the library, the first thing I do is to hand in my book to the librarian and then, after consulting the card index, I look for my book on the shelves.

Put equal quantities of powdered alum, salt and chalk into three separate test-tubes and then pour into each tube equal quantities of water and then shake the tubes well and it will then be found that the salt dissolves quickly and the alum after a short time, and the chalk does not appear to dissolve at all.

Put equal quantities of powdered alum, salt and chalk into three separate test-tubes. Pour into each tube equal quantities of water and shake the tubes well. It will be found that the salt dissolves quickly and the alum after a short time, but that the chalk does not dissolve at all.

EXERCISES

1. Rewrite the following passages in an improved way, by avoiding the unnecessary use of *and* and *then*:

(*a*) Then, about 4 o'clock, the people begin to go home, and the stallholders pack up their stalls, and then the roads and pavements are swept and so the market is once more deserted.

(*b*) As there is a growing interest in swimming in our club, I have been asked to write to you about arranging a competition between our two clubs, and if you are agreeable, I suggest that we two meet and then we can discuss the arrangements for the competition.

(*c*) A school can help its pupils to choose a career by

taking groups of boys round some of the local factories, and in this way the boys can form their own opinions, and the school can also show films of the different kinds of work in the neighbourhood.

(*d*) I ran downstairs and then ate my breakfast, and after grabbing my bag I dashed out of the hotel in which I had stayed the night, and then I made my way quickly to the bus stop.

(*e*) I then opened the largest parcel with very great care, and as I opened it a pair of wheels caught my eye and then another pair, and finally to my surprise I found myself the owner of an electric train, and I nearly cried with joy.

(*f*) These sales are great occasions among the people of the hills and everyone attends them, and there is much hospitality and a good deal of business is transacted, and there are many meetings of old friends.

(*g*) The father of Josiah Wedgwood was a poor potter at Burslem, barely able to make a living at his trade, and he died when Josiah was only eleven years old, and at that early age Josiah began to work as a thrower at his elder brother's wheel.

(*h*) He started out as a doctor in a whaling ship and then for a short time he was a medical officer in the Navy, and afterwards he had a good practice in Valparaiso and the last I heard of him was that he had settled in Singapore.

(*i*) Lay the outer surface of the bandage over the right groin, then pass the bandage round the thigh and carry it up over the front of the right groin to the left hip, round the back and right hip, and then over the lower part of the abdomen to the outer side of the left thigh.

(*j*) About 6 o'clock I returned to my flat, changed and then went out to dine at a restaurant in King Street. I then spent a couple of enjoyable hours at our local music-hall. Then after a snack at a coffee-bar I again returned to my flat, and that is, John, how I spent the evening.

(*k*) My friend told me that Mr. Martin had been collecting books for nearly 40 years and took great pride in his library, and when strangers visited his house it was difficult for him to refrain from pointing out to them some of his most valuable acquisitions, and even if the visitors were more addicted to television than to the reading of books, they were not allowed to escape from what was one of Mr. Martin's greatest pleasures.

(1) The mice held a meeting to consider what they should do to protect themselves from the cat and though several plans were discussed, none of them was regarded as satisfactory, and then a young mouse proposed that a bell should be hung round the cat's neck and the result would be that when the bell sounded and they heard the cat coming they would all have the time to run back into their holes.

2. The following passages contain too many short sentences. Rewrite the passages so that they run more smoothly.

(*a*) Edward Fitzgerald was born near Woodbridge, Suffolk, in 1809. He was the seventh of eight children. His father was a typical country squire, fond of hunting and shooting. He was M.P. for Seaford. Fitzgerald's mother was a gifted woman, a good linguist and fond of poetry. Edward was educated at King Edward's School, Bury St. Edmunds. At the age of 17, he entered Trinity College, Cambridge. There he was a contemporary of Thackeray.

(*b*) I was about half-way to my home. I heard a strange noise behind me. It was something between a snore and a growl. It terrified me and made me fear for my life. I came to the conclusion that some strange creature was not far from me. As I could see nothing, I hastened on my way. Suddenly the sound was repeated, but this time it was louder and more menacing than before. My heart stood still. It flashed across my mind that some strange beast must surely be after me.

(*c*) When Alexander was a small lad, a Thessalian offered to sell his father, Philip of Macedon, a horse. Unfortunately, the horse was so vicious and unmanageable that no one could mount it. Philip, therefore, ordered the man to take it back. Alexander had been watching the proceedings. He asked permission to try the horse himself. Alexander noticed that the horse shied at its own shadow. He turned it to the sun, spoke gently to it and stroked its back. He then leapt lightly up and set it going at full gallop. The king and court were in terror. They feared for the prince's life. When he returned in safety, Philip embraced him. He said to his son: "Seek another kingdom, my son, for Macedonia is too small for you."

(*d*) The sport-loving citizens of Terrydene, California, seemed to Orinski to be fair-minded men. They seemed to him to be impartial and free from bias. Though he was a foreigner, he was given a rousing reception as he climbed into the ring. Such is the tonic effect of applause, he felt his depression lifting and almost vanishing. He had good reason to be depressed. Here he was in a strange country — a foreigner with very little knowledge of the language. He had, in addition, no relatives or friends to comfort him. His opponent, too, had the reputation of being merciless in attack. Orinski decided, however, not to sacrifice himself meekly. He would show that he was a man of mettle and determination. He would show his opponent that he could give as well as receive.

III

PUNCTUATION

Punctuation is of the utmost importance in making clear the meaning of what we write. The omission or the misuse of stops can cause confusion or obscurity or ambiguity, and hinder the rapid understanding of the ideas we wish to convey to the reader.

1. Apostrophe

Misuse of the apostrophe is widespread. The apostrophe is used to show: (*a*) possession (possessive case); (*b*) that one or more letters have been omitted.

(*a*) *To Denote Possession*

There are three main rules:

(i) Add an apostrophe *s* ('*s*) in the singular:

the boy's books	= the books of (*or* belonging to) the boy
the hero's exploits	= the exploits of the hero
the princess's jewels	= the jewels of the princess
Charles's house	= the house of Charles
St. Paul's Cathedral	= the Cathedral of St. Paul

(ii) If the plural does not end in *s*, add an apostrophe *s* ('*s*) as in the singular:

the women's coats	= the coats of the women
the workmen's tools	= the tools of the workmen

(iii) If the plural ends in *s*, add an apostrophe ('):

the ladies' hats	= the hats of the ladies
the princesses' jewels	= the jewels of the princesses
the thieves' haul	= the haul of the thieves
the heroes' exploits	= the exploits of the heroes
the teachers' room	= the room of the teachers

Study the following additional examples of the use of the apostrophe:

one week's holiday	two weeks' holiday
one's leisure hours	to cross the t's
in ten minutes' time	Gilbert and Sullivan's operas
John Galsworthy's and G. B. Shaw's plays	the M.P.'s constituency
	the two J.P.s' secretaries

Note. Do not put an apostrophe in the following pronouns: *yours, theirs, whose, ours, hers, oneself.*

EXERCISE

Write down the possessive form of the following:

e.g.	the friend of my wife	my wife's friend
	the books of his sisters	his sisters' books

leave of absence for one month; the magazine of the students; the novels of H. G. Wells; at the pace of a snail; *Barnaby Rudge* by Charles Dickens; the house of his brother-in-law; pensions for widows; after a delay of three hours; the son of my hostess; in the time of my grandparents; a meeting of directors; the summing-up of the judge; notice of six months; the speech by the Foreign Minister; the decision of the delegates; the cigarettes of the two N.C.O.s; the answers of the chieftain; the poetry of Byron and of Shelley; the tales of the travellers; the heroism of an apprentice; the gallery for peeresses; from the viewpoint of the spectators and of the players; the brochure of the travel agent; the quarrels of the men-servants.

(*b*) *To Denote Omission*

The following examples show the use of the apostrophe to indicate the omission of one or more letters:

shouldn't	=should not	I'm	=I am
can't	=cannot	don't	=do not
who'll	=who will	won't	=will not
it's	=it is	who's	=who is

EXERCISES

1. Where necessary, insert the apostrophe in the following sentences:

(*a*) Arent you going for a walk?
(*b*) They wont accept our invitation.
(*c*) Weve won the trophy.
(*d*) Theres the boy whos going to win the race.
(*e*) He doesnt understand why hes not been promoted.
(*f*) Its not yours; its ours.
(*g*) We werent told whose plane it was.
(*h*) Id like to know why they dont write to us.
(*i*) If the books not yours, lets find its owner.
(*j*) You musnt end a letter to a friend with "Yours faithfully".

2. Where necessary, insert the apostrophe in the following expressions:

my cake and Johns; a nine days wonder; the tigresss cubs; a dogs home; to his hearts content; the bosns whistle; St Thomass Hospital; other workers overalls; the monkeys paw; the workpeoples entrance; travellers cheques; to mind your ps and qs.

a stones throw; womens magazines; after three hours search; out of harms way; my nieces book; most tobacconists shops; 3rd class at Lloyds; the housewives outing;

at his fingers ends; the two artists impressions; because of someone elses fault; our familys income.

Her Majestys Stationery Office; for goodness sake; their parents money; another head teachers position; at the newsagents on the platform; birds eggs; near the focsle; Thomson & Co.s offices; the amplification of the actors and actresses voices; in seven years time; a girls boarding-school; on ones own merits.

2. Confusion in Use between Full Stop and Comma

(*a*) *Sentences*

Most students know that the end of a sentence is marked by a full stop (sometimes by a question mark or an exclamation mark), not by a comma. One can have very little sympathy, therefore, with candidates who, in writing a paragraph of about ten lines, put no mark of punctuation at all, or a comma instead of a full stop, at the end of one or more of the sentences. Students at this stage should have learnt where a sentence ends and a new one begins, and be able to insert full stops correctly in a passage of their own composition.

Do not write sentences of the following type, where two sentences are regarded as clauses and are separated by a comma:

> I saw that the ladies were very tired and hungry, I offered them some of the food that we had stored away in case of emergency. (Wrong)
>
> The mansion was up for sale, the owners could no longer afford to maintain it in its present condition. (Wrong)

The two sentences in each of these examples should be joined by a conjunction to form one longer sentence:

As I saw that the ladies were very tired and hungry, I offered them some of the food that we had stored away in case of emergency. (Correct)

The mansion was up for sale, because the owners could no longer afford to maintain it in its present condition. (Correct)

See page 12.

EXERCISES

1. Combine, by using a conjunction, each of the following pairs of sentences into one longer sentence:

(*a*) Last night, a stone was thrown through your bedroom window, it was whilst you were out for a walk.

(*b*) My friend not only passed in all four subjects to qualify for admission to the college, she was also awarded a scholarship tenable for three years.

(*c*) This gave me a splendid chance for a shoulder shot at about fifty yards' distance, I knelt down at once and fired after taking careful aim.

(*d*) You may resent what I am going to say, nevertheless I propose to speak the truth.

(*e*) Much as I wanted to add a giraffe to my collection of trophies, I left the animals undisturbed, I think it a pity to shoot these rather rare and very harmless creatures.

(*f*) He has a very bad temper and can be most rude, he has, however, great courage and is a man of the highest integrity.

(*g*) Joan was terrified when she heard what seemed to be a cry for help, she was much relieved to find a little later that her fears had been groundless.

(*h*) We must stick to our various jobs, we must always be on the look-out for new opportunities of spreading good cheer and of lending a helping hand.

(*i*) The new boy in our form had never been taught how to do simultaneous equations, John Payne, the boy sitting next to him, volunteered to give him a lesson or two on the subject.

(*j*) We went by boat to Nice, we stayed there for a fortnight and arrived home the day before we were due to return to school.

2. Where necessary, substitute full stops for commas and capital letters for small letters in the following passages:

(*a*) Kenneth had never met his grandfather before, and he gazed in astonishment at him, he had met old people before, but he had not thought that anything quite so old as Grandfather Crooke had ever existed or ever could exist, he was little, and wrinkled, and shrivelled, and bald.

(*b*) Beryl on tiptoe went off into the galley, closing the door carefully behind her, she knew, like Captain Stone, and all the others, that Terence was right, there were more urgent things to think of than the red-haired boy, they were still in the fog.

(*c*) Walter had very little difficulty in finding the dining-hall, he was guided there by the smell of cooking and the sound of voices, it was a large, panelled room, far from disagreeable, with fifty or sixty boys of ages ranging from ten to eighteen settled along four long tables, the smaller boys wore Eton suits, the elder ones dinner-jackets.

(*d*) After a period, during which I sat in bewilderment, I set myself to try to discover what sudden misfortune could have befallen my comrades, the whole disordered appearance of the camp showed that there had been some sort of attack, and the rifle-shot no doubt marked the time when it had occurred, that there should have been only one shot showed that it had all been over in an instant, the rifles still lay on the ground, and one of them — Harold Watson's — had the empty cartridge in the breech.

(*e*) The hangar was made of wood with a corrugated iron roof, it was like a garage to look at, only a bit bigger, there was a drift, knee-deep, against the door, which they soon cleared, a twist of the key in the lock, a heave together, and one of the doors clanked open, behold inside the Hornet Moth, a snug fit, with her wings folded back and a good thickness of felt roped about the nose.

(*b*) *Phrases and Clauses*

A phrase or a subordinate clause must not be treated as the equivalent of a sentence:

> The art gallery contains many beautiful English portraits. Ranging from the days of Elizabeth to our own time.

"Ranging . . . time" is not a complete sentence; it cannot stand alone; it has no finite verb; it is not even a clause, but an adjectival phrase qualifying "many beautiful English portraits".

The sentence should be written:

> The art gallery contains many beautiful English portraits, ranging from the days of Elizabeth to our own time.

> As we are very busy this week, I cannot give you permission to leave work at 4 p.m. Though I may, in view of your difficult home circumstances, let you leave early from next Monday.

"Though I may . . . from next Monday" is not a sentence, but an adverbial clause of concession modifying "cannot give" in the main clause.

The sentence should be written:

> As we are very busy this week, I cannot give you permission to leave work at 4 p.m., though I may, in view of your difficult home circumstances, let you leave early from next Monday.

EXERCISE

Where necessary, substitute commas for full stops and small letters for capital letters in the following passages:

(*a*) I regret that I cannot accept your invitation. The reason being that I have already made arrangements to spend a week-end at my uncle's house in the country.

(*b*) Our mathematics text-books cover a very wide field. Extending from simple arithmetic for pupils in the first form to trigonometry for those in the fifth.

(*c*) There are a very large number of libraries in this country. Most of which contain books of especial interest to technical students.

(*d*) Our school fared very badly in their football matches against our competitors in the Mortavian League. Because we were handicapped throughout the season by the illness of one of our best players.

(*e*) Bob Loveday introduced himself to Captain Hardy as the son of the miller of Overcombe. To which the Captain replied that he knew Bob's father well.

(*f*) I am very sorry indeed to part from all the friends I have made since I came to this school nearly seven years ago. The friends with whom I have shared the joys and sorrows of school life.

(*g*) John Sargent was Cornish by birth. His parents having come from Truro to Devonport for business reasons when John was eight years old.

(*h*) The writer stated that different people had different opinions. An example being the townsman's and the countryman's attitude towards the land.

(*i*) Stephen is keenly interested in his school work and came first in IVA in the recent Midsummer examination. Whereas Paul is weak in academic subjects and took 24th place out of 32 boys in IVB.

(*j*) Although the two boys protested that they had paid for their seats and that they were not the only ones who had been shouting. The manager told them that they would be sent out of the cinema the next time they disturbed the other members of the audience.

3. Confusion in Use between Semicolon and Comma

Do not separate by a comma two or more co-ordinate clauses in a sentence such as the following. Use a full stop, or a semicolon if the clauses are closely linked in sense.

> English is the basis of literacy; it is the only medium of instruction in the classroom; it infiltrates into every other subject of the curriculum; it has great social value; it is the key to self-education after we leave school.

There are five co-ordinate clauses in this sentence, all of them closely linked in sense. It would be wrong, therefore, to put commas after *literacy*, *classroom*, *curriculum*, and *value*.

Note the use of the semicolon in the following sentences:

> It gave her quite a shock to see how old he looked; she thought that his careworn features made him more suitable for the part of a sexagenarian than that of a young hero.

> I did not spend many years at school; I had to leave at the age of eleven in order to start work and make my contribution to the running of the household.

> I do not remember any time in my career when I was so satisfied with my lot; even today the memory of the year I spent working on a farm gives me great pleasure.

> When Clifford suddenly appeared on the scene with two native policemen, he looked a sorry sight; his spectacles

were broken; he had a black eye and a nasty gash across his forehead; his collar hung loosely and was swinging in the breeze; and his clothes seemed as if they had accumulated the dust of centuries.

EXERCISE

Where necessary, substitute full stops or semicolons for the commas, and capital letters for the small letters, in the following passages:

(*a*) After leaving Cambridge I came across a man who was leading an expedition to Brazil, he asked me to go with him.

(*b*) Some years ago you used to teach me how to play the piano, do you remember?

(*c*) Paul stood next to Mrs. Dampier, she had on her Sunday bonnet and a black veil, he wore his best suit, a white shirt and a black tie.

(*d*) The Speaker of the House of Commons sees that every point of view has a chance of being expressed, the Lord Chancellor acts as Speaker of the House of Lords.

(*e*) I have decided to have my meals alone in future, will you tell the servants? It makes me feel ill to talk so much.

(*f*) Every journalist knows the value of "exclusive" news, people talk about it, readers of other newspapers are attracted to what they regard as the more enterprising newspaper.

(*g*) I soon realised that the current criticism of Dickens was nonsense, he did not make a caricature of people, he simply let me see them more than life size.

(*h*) As he peered down, he saw a procession emerge from a door and move slowly across the hall to a door opposite, he laughed loudly, well did he know what the procession meant.

(*i*) Madge went out and did housework, Phyllis, the pretty one, was driven to do the same, in spite of protests, Tom drove a delivery-waggon, and Fred went to school, no matter how hungry they all might be, Fred must have his schooling, because he was the "smart" one.

(*j*) Cecil Rhodes said *The Story of an African Farm* "enraptured him", he was "unable to account for its splendour", again and again he referred to the concluding chapters as "masterpieces", and to the book itself as a work of "profound genius".

4. Quotation Marks or Inverted Commas

(*a*) *Transition from Direct to Reported Speech* (*Indirect Speech*)

Do not use inverted commas when you turn a passage from direct to reported speech:

Direct. The boy said, "I shall not be going to the cinema this evening."

Reported. The boy said that, "he would not be going to the cinema that evening." (Wrong)

The words in inverted commas do not repeat the actual words of the speaker. The comma after *that* is wrong.

The boy said that he would not be going to the cinema that evening. (Correct)

Here is another example:

Direct. "Have you the time, John, to help me with a difficult crossword puzzle?" asked Sheila.

Indirect. Sheila asked John whether "he had the time to help her with a difficult crossword puzzle." (Wrong)

Sheila asked John whether he had the time to help her with a difficult crossword puzzle. (Correct)

(*b*) *Quotation within a Quotation*

Examine the quotation marks in the following passage:

> A. H. Clough, at the close of 1853, wrote to C. E. Norton: "I send you M. Arnold's poems. I myself think 'The Scholar Gipsy' is the best. It is *so* true to the Oxford country."

The three sentences beginning with "I send you" and ending with "the Oxford country" are placed within double inverted commas because they repeat the exact words of the writer. Normally, *The Scholar Gipsy*, the name of the poem, would have been written "The Scholar Gipsy", but as we have already used double inverted commas, we now use single inverted commas and write 'The Scholar Gipsy'.

The following further examples illustrate the use of single inverted commas:

> His friend replied: "I prefer 'David Copperfield' to 'Oliver Twist', as the character of Bill Sykes does not appeal to me."
>
> "Take heed," said Bob's father, "of the saying of Edison: 'Genius is 2 per cent. inspiration and 98 per cent. perspiration.' "
>
> "Do not forget," said the senior prefect, "what Sir Henry Newbolt wrote in his poem 'Vitaï Lampada': 'Play up! play up! and play the game!' "

EXERCISE

Where necessary, complete the punctuation of the following sentences by the addition of inverted commas: (There are two sentences in which no inverted commas are required.)

(*a*) Destroyer astern! shouted the officer in the submarine.

(*b*) Come home from school as quickly as you can, said Richard's uncle, as I want you to help me in the garden.

(*c*) The patrol leader said that they would probably reach Addington at 4 o'clock.

(*d*) Macbeth is the most important character in Shakespeare's Macbeth.

(*e*) The following lines are from Tennyson's Morte d'Arthur:

And answer made the bold Sir Bedivere:
I heard the ripple washing in the reeds,
And the wild water lapping on the crag.

(*f*) This applicant states in his letter that he is one of the representatives of a leading commercial firm in Norway.

(*g*) Marco was much surprised when the fat man said meekly: Yes, I have been to Cathay; and it took me three years to get there.

(*h*) When I spoke to him, said Maggie, about the loss of the parcel, all he answered was My fault entirely.

(*i*) Thank goodness the engine did start, said Maud, and then, in a happier voice, she said, I'm going to light the stove now, and we'll have the rest of our breakfast.

(*j*) I am going to read to you, said the headmaster, one of the most quoted speeches in Shakespeare's plays — the speech beginning All the world's a stage in As You Like It.

5. Change of Meaning

A change in punctuation may cause a complete change in the meaning of a sentence. Compare the sentences in each of the following pairs:

The doctor says John prefers the theatre to the cinema.

"The doctor," says John, "prefers the theatre to the cinema."

A pass is required in English, history and economics.

A pass is required in English history and economics.

EXERCISES

1. Change the punctuation but not the wording of the following sentences, so that each sentence has another meaning:

(*a*) Very few people I know have such a command of the English language as our local M.P.

(*b*) Where can I buy a hat like this one in Edinburgh?

(*c*) Call him, George, and see whether he answers.

(*d*) The adjudicators had to listen to twenty-three minute speeches.

(*e*) Harold left for Dublin at six o'clock.

(*f*) The groundsman says Mr. Lennox is the best footballer in the village.

(*g*) Alfred the schoolkeeper's nephew has been promoted to the rank of captain.

(*h*) This picture was painted for £100 more than I am likely to receive for it in the sale.

(*i*) What does Mrs. Timson want you to pay for the use of her typewriter?

(*j*) After running home from school very quickly, he told his brother how he had scored his first century.

2. Two marks of punctuation have been omitted from each of the following sentences. Rewrite the sentences correctly.

(*a*) It took him a long time to realise, as he came from a totalitarian state that the peoples rights in this country were safeguarded by Act of Parliament.

(*b*) The witness stated that he was a 26-year old factory worker and that he was earning £15 a week.

(*c*) His inventiveness not inferior, I think, to Picasso's amounted to genius.

(*d*) Thomas Sheridan was the father of the dramatist who wrote "The Rivals and The School for Scandal".

(*e*) Would you like me to have a talk with your father Robert, and see what I can do for you

(*f*) Her work in France took her from one part of the country to the other her work in Ireland was a great success her work in Italy was admired both by aristocrat and by peasant.

(*g*) Please let me have the following as soon as possible three rolls, four packets of tea, a pint of vinegar a jar of pickles.

(*h*) "I enjoyed reading," he said, "Sir Walter Scott's Rob Roy."

(*i*) "Look" she cried as the deep stretch of grass that had seemed so dreamily peaceful leapt into life.

(*j*) "Its not my purpose," he said, "to lecture this evening on the negroes attitude to this question."

3. Complete the punctuation of the following passage:

CAPTAIN. What are you going to do when you leave school Alfred

ALFRED. My parents intend to put me with Jones & Mortice they hope that one day I ll become the manager of a department.

CAPTAIN. Thats no life for a man you ought to go to sea what do you think

ALFRED. I d like to go to sea very much sir I dont want to go into an office.

CAPTAIN. Set your mind at rest Alfred I feel sure that your father will see reason after I have pointed out to him the advantages of a career at sea.

4. Punctuate the following passages, add the necessary capitals, and set out the passages correctly:

(*a*) will you have a glass of wine with me sir said the ambassador the duke held up a protesting hand thank you i never touch it i have to be careful very careful with my digestion

(*b*) the stewardess surveyed the twins and her smile deepened i hope you both enjoy the voyage in fact im sure you will now have you everything you want yes thank you answered the twins together

(*c*) hello said amelia glancing at the opened letter which lay near nigels elbow who is that from its from cristopher redburn he replied oh and what has he to say she asked nothing he answered hm sneered amelia it must be a very funny letter if its about nothing

(*d*) after breakfast next morning edwin surveyed the cleared area good work farmer giles he said quizzically what do you propose planting groundnuts but not all groundnuts surely what can you do with them anyway youd be surprised they can be used for margarine soap and cattle food why do you know went on farmer giles warming to the subject a scientist recently discovered no fewer than three hundred substances in groundnuts

(*e*) good evening said he with a friendly smile im just going to have my coffee wont you have a cup too bickers mr bickers took no notice of this hospitable invitation but closed the door behind him and said i want a few words with you mr railsford certainly ive nothing to do wont you take a seat mr bickers took a seat a little disconcerted by railsfords determined good humour he had not counted upon that the last time i saw you you were hardly so polite said he with a sneer when was that im very sorry if i was rude i had no intention i assure you

IV

VOCABULARY

1. Malapropisms

Mrs Malaprop, a character in *The Rivals* by R. B. Sheridan, frequently blunders in her use of words — often with ludicrous results — by confusing the meaning of two words that have a slight resemblance to each other in sound:

> Oh, it gives me the *hydrostatics* to such a degree. I thought she had *persisted* from corresponding with him; but, behold, this very day I have *interceded* another letter from this fellow.

Mrs Malaprop has confused *hydrostatics* with *hysterics*, *persisted* with *desisted*, and *interceded* with *intercepted*.

Candidates provide examiners with a plentiful supply of malapropisms.

EXERCISES

1. Write down the words that should have been used in place of the words in italics in the sentences below.

2. Introduce each of the words *in italics* into a sentence to show that you understand its meaning.

(*a*) I should like to visit Norway to see the *glaziers*.

(*b*) Fishing is a joy to every *Anglican*.

(*c*) He was accused of *deformation* of character.

(*d*) I saw a number of *deceased* beggars at the corner of the street.

(*e*) Successful *anecdotes* have been discovered to most poisons.

(*f*) We were glad to hear from my sister that she had arrived safely at her *destiny*.

(*g*) The situation must be viewed in its true *prospective*.

(*h*) My friend was admitted to a mental *constitution*.

(*i*) When he was attacked by a lion, he sought *sanction* in a tree.

(*j*) My teacher is the very *epistle* of kindness.

(*k*) An *arbitrary* committee should be set up to *meditate* between employers and employees.

(*l*) The people living at the present time are more *venerable* to *cosmetic* radiation than those in the past.

2. Synonyms

Synonyms are words that are similar in meaning. They are not interchangeable; they may approximate in meaning and use, but a shade of difference always remains: e.g. *crowd*, *mob*, *audience*, *congregation*. We associate each of these four words with a gathering of people; but a *mob* suggests uproar or violence or lawlessness, as opposed to the peaceful gathering of people in a *crowd*; an *audience*, a gathering of people to see a play at a theatre or a film at a cinema, or to listen to a speech; a *congregation*, a gathering of people in a place of worship. You must therefore know the *exact* meaning of synonymous words in order to avoid using them in unsuitable contexts.

The following sentences illustrate the use of these four words as nouns:

> The large *crowd* outside Buckingham Palace cheered again and again when the Royal Family came out on to the balcony.

The Bastille was completely destroyed by the *mob* in 1789.

Some members of the *audience* expressed their dissatisfaction with the play because the villain married the heroine and the hero was unjustly punished.

The small country church seldom had a *congregation* of more than 30, either in summer or in winter.

The following examples show the difference in meaning of four synonyms (*renew*, *restore*, *refresh*, *renovate*) used as verbs:

renew — to make new again or like new something in a poor condition:

My wife *renewed* the lining in my old jacket.

restore — to bring back to a former condition or its original state:

A month's holiday in Switzerland *restored* the comedian to health.

refresh — to bring back lost strength, etc.:

The two children were very much *refreshed* by the cool drink they bought at the stall.

renovate — to make new again, but usually limited to material things such as a house, a motor-car, furniture, etc.:

The upholsterer is coming to *renovate* the chairs in our lounge.

The following synonyms used as adjectives are treated below in a similar way: *old*, *ancient*, *antiquated*, *obsolete*:

old — having lived long or existed long; not young or new:

Thomas Hardy was an *old* man when he wrote *The Tragedy of the Queen of Cornwall.*

ancient — belonging to a time in the distant past; not modern:

The archaeologist was rewarded for his patience by his discovery of the first *ancient* tomb to be found intact.

antiquated — out-of-date:

His *antiquated* ideas on the upbringing of children made him unfitted to be the father of two boys.

obsolete — no longer in use:

Many words that were current in Shakespeare's time are now *obsolete.*

EXERCISES

1. Write down *two* synonyms for each of the following words:

cunning, amaze, courage, salary, storm, abbreviate, assist, gigantic, despondent, compassion, ability, predict, cheerful, contemplate, instruct, increase, pleasure, famous, hazardous, odious.

2. Choose the correct word from the two words in brackets to complete the following sentences, and introduce the other word into a sentence to show that you understand its meaning and use:

(*a*) If my friend had taken the tenth commandment to heart, he would not have been so (*covetous*, *avaricious*) of the pony my father gave me as a birthday present.

(*b*) Paul (*slandered*, *libelled*) his employer in an article he wrote for the local paper.

(*c*) "You are a (*trespasser*, *intruder*) on my property," said the farmer.

(*d*) As a (*symbol*, *token*) of our esteem for the chairman, we presented him with a tea-service.

(*e*) The (*hospitable*, *benevolent*) old gentleman who lives across the road has given another £50 towards the equipment of our club.

(*f*) Complaints were made that the new apprentice was (*hindering*, *obstructing*) several other apprentices in their work.

(*g*) The manager promised that the hall would be (*adorned*, *decorated*) before the arrival of the guests.

(*h*) This food has been found on analysis to be (*defective*, *deficient*) in vitamins.

(*i*) He was granted (*exemption*, *immunity*) from the preliminary examination as he had passed in English and three other subjects.

(*j*) Though my son is weak in academic subjects, he is more (*intellectual*, *intelligent*) than most of the other boys in his class.

3. Distinguish in meaning between the words in each of the following pairs and introduce each word into a sentence to illustrate its use:

habit, custom; aged, elderly; shrewd, cunning; poverty, misery; construct, manufacture; peculiar, mysterious; tour, excursion; replace, substitute; cure, remedy; riot, revolution; character, reputation; reduce, contract.

4. Use each of the following words in a sentence to show that you understand the difference in meaning of the words in each group:

(*a*) wise, learned, clever;
(*b*) abandon, withdraw, discard;
(*c*) honest, trustworthy, honourable;
(*d*) friend, companion, acquaintance, comrade;
(*e*) recite, rehearse, relate, recapitulate;
(*f*) hobby, amusement, pastime, recreation.

3. Homophones

These words have the same sound but differ in spelling and meaning: e.g. *board*, *bored; cue*, *queue; plain*, *plane*. Students who are weak in spelling often confuse the words in pairs of this kind.

See page 2.

EXERCISES

1. Write down one homophone for each of the following:

ascent, serial, serge, magnet, signet, bail, birth, maize, cast, stake, beach, ceiling, cord, pour, veil, border, colonel, muscle, team, whale, taught, check, bolder, guilt.

2. Compose sentences, one sentence for each word, to show that you understand the difference in meaning between the words in each of the following pairs:

stationary, stationery; metal, mettle; pedal, peddle; canvas, canvass; lightning, lightening; principal, principle; brooch, broach; incite, insight; compliment, complement; martial, marshal; populous, populace; council, counsel.

4. Confusion of Words

Besides homophones, there are many other words (some of them very simple) that are sometimes confused:

e.g. *lend, borrow; human, humane; affect, effect.*

We *lend to* a person but *borrow from* a person.

Human means "of man", "of mankind":

Human nature has not changed much despite our scientific and technological progress.

Humane means "kind", "compassionate":

We expected her to be more *humane* in dealing with the domestic problems of the female staff.

Affect is a verb and cannot be used as a noun. It has two meanings: (i) "to assume", "to make a pretence of":

It seems strange to me that Herbert should *affect* such an air of superiority merely because he has inherited a sum of money.

(ii) "to have an effect on", "to be moved by":

My year's service as an engineer in the tropics has *affected* my health.

He was very much *affected* by the distress and misery he saw in some of the under-developed countries.

Effect can be used (i) as a noun, meaning "result", "influence":

The drug had an immediate *effect* upon him.

(ii) as a verb, meaning "to bring about", "to accomplish":

Our troops *effected* a landing on the enemy's coast.

EXERCISES

1. Distinguish in meaning between the words in each of the following pairs:

rout, route; statue, statute; rare, unique; deduct, deduce; illegible, eligible; allusion, illusion; uninterested, disinterested; elicit, illicit; masterly, masterful; observance, observation; respectful, respectable; sceptic, septic; industrial, industrious; urban, urbane; affection, affectation; definite, definitive.

2. Compose sentences, one sentence for each word, to show that you understand the difference in meaning between the words in each of the following pairs:

compose, comprise; alternate, alternative; infer, imply; historic, historical; practical, practicable; economic, economical; imaginary, imaginative; continual, continuous; official, officious; judicial, judicious; exhausting, exhaustive; credible, credulous; amend, emend; adverse, averse; ingenious, ingenuous; progress, progression.

5. Misuse of Words

Many words in the English language are frequently misused:

e.g. *aggravate, transpire, anticipate.*

The colloquial use of *aggravate* in the sense of "annoy" should be avoided in writing. *Aggravate* means "make worse":

Alice aggravates me every time she comes into the house. (Wrong)

Distress in Ireland in the 1840s was *aggravated* by a potato famine. (Correct)

Transpire does not mean "happen", but "become known", "leak out":

I was a witness of the fight that transpired at the dance hall last night. (Wrong)

It *transpired* at the trial that the prisoner had been convicted twice before for a similar offence. (Correct)

Anticipate does not mean the same as "expect":

We anticipate that the game will start at 4 p.m. (Wrong)

It is correctly used in the sense of "forestall" (person or thing) or "foresee":

Anticipating a complaint from his next-door neighbours, he told the children playing in the garden not to make so much noise. (Correct)

The Government spokesman said that he could not *anticipate* the measures that would be taken to combat the menace. (Correct)

EXERCISES

1. Introduce each of the following words into a sentence to show that you understand its correct use:

nice, individual, mutual, literally, terrible, resource, enhance, protagonist, virtually, respectively, awful, percentage, partake, decimate, partially, minimise, feasible, frightful, relatively, majority, intriguing, sensational, stupendous, appalling, chronic, colossal, biennial, adequate, alibi.

2. Explain clearly the difference in meaning between the expressions in each of the following pairs:

(*a*) a *brief* reply and a *concise* reply; a *dutiful* child and a *respectful* child; a *boring* story and an *uninteresting* story; a *probable* solution and a *possible* solution; a *deceitful* person and a *dishonest* person; an *unknown* custom and an *unfamiliar* custom; a *qualified* instructor and a *competent* instructor; a *famous* pianist and a *brilliant* pianist; a *sarcastic* remark and an *ironical* remark; a *false* statement and an *inaccurate* statement.

(*b*) to display *skill* and to display *ingenuity*; the cause of the *misunderstanding* and the cause of the *dispute*; to be present at a *discussion* and to be present at a *debate*; a great *misfortune* and a great *disaster*; in a strange *language* and in a strange *dialect*; the next *campaign* and the next *battle*; an *advertisement* in the newspaper and an *announcement* in the newspaper; with his usual *courtesy* and with his usual *humility*; a serious *offence* and a serious *fault*; to take part in a *pageant* and to take part in a *procession*.

(*c*) to *protect* from danger and to *rescue* from danger; to *print* a novel and to *publish* a novel; to *condemn* for his action and to *despise* for his action; to *ridicule* an opponent and to *taunt* an opponent; to *defy* a referee and to *threaten* a referee; to *seize* a toy pistol and to *confiscate* a toy pistol; to *blame* for the loss and to *censure* for the loss; to be *appointed* prefect and to be *elected* prefect; to *destroy* the property and to *demolish* the property; to *inspect* the machine and to *overhaul* the machine.

V

AGREEMENT OF VERB AND SUBJECT

A verb must agree with its subject in number and person.

1. Articles

When two singular nouns form the subject of a sentence and are both preceded by the definite or the indefinite article, the verb is in the plural:

The poet and the dramatist *have* returned from exile.

Note that in this sentence the poet and the dramatist are two separate persons.

Compare the following sentence:

Shakespeare, the great poet and dramatist, *was* born in 1564.

Here the poet and dramatist is one and the same person.

Compare also the following sentences:

A black and a white horse *have* been offered for sale.
A black and white horse *has* been offered for sale.

The verb is in the plural in the first sentence because there are two horses for sale; in the singular in the second, because there is only one horse for sale.

2. *And*

When two singular nouns, or the equivalent of two singular nouns, are connected by *and* and form the subject of a sentence, the verb is in the plural:

Mary and I *are* going for a walk.

Stephen and your brother *have* not been late this term.

If the two singular nouns, however, are intended to convey a single idea, the verb is in the singular as the subject is then singular in sense:

Part and parcel of his work *is* to decipher telegrams in code.

The horse and cart *was* originally used to take my fruit to market.

3. Number and Person

Remember that the general rule applies in all cases: the verb agrees with its subject in number and person.

(*a*) A singular subject with an enlargement is followed by a singular verb:

The tape recorder with its accessories *has* been missing since Sunday.

Many students go astray by treating *accessories* as the subject instead of regarding it as part of the enlargement.

Here are two further examples:

A *slide-rule* with its case *has* been removed from my table.

"With its case", the enlargement of the subject, is an adjectival phrase qualifying the subject "slide-rule", which is singular and therefore followed by the singular verb "has". *With*, unlike *and*, is a preposition, not a conjunction.

In a similar way, the subject *box* is followed by the singular *is* in the following sentence:

This unique *box* as well as its contents *is* on view to the public.

Compare the following:

A slide-rule *and* its case *have* been removed from my table.

This unique box *and* its contents *are* on view to the public.

The following additional examples should be studied carefully:

The *cat* as well as its kittens *has* had no food this morning.

His *knowledge* of several European languages, together with his ability to express himself clearly and concisely, *was* mainly responsible for his rapid promotion.

Nothing but wild land thickly overgrown with trees and bushes *was* visible to the pilot of the machine.

There *were*, including the speaker, the chairman and the secretary, only eighteen *people* present when the president of the society arrived.

This *magazine comes* out every Friday and *costs* one shilling.

(*b*) The verb must agree with its subject not only in number but also in person:

I as well as my daughters *am* sailing for the United States. (1st person)

You as well as he *are* to leave the house immediately. (2nd person)

Charles together with his three friends *has* started out on an expedition to the interior of Brazil. (3rd person)

(*c*) In sentences with *not only . . . but also*, the verb takes the number and person of the second subject:

Not only James, but also the native *workmen were* fast asleep.
=Not only (was) James (fast asleep), but also . . . .

Not only you, but also your *brother has* worried me twice this week.
=Not only (have) you (worried me twice this week), but also . . . .

EXERCISES

1. Insert one of the following words in the blank spaces: *am*, *is*, *are*, *was*, *were*, *has*, *have:*

(*a*) A prefect, together with eleven boys from our form, — herded into one compartment.

(*b*) Two books as well as a penknife — presented to me on my birthday.

(*c*) Our representative in Cairo, with his wife, son and two daughters, — returning to England next July.

(*d*) Not only the walls, but also the ceiling — blackened by soot.

(*e*) The lack of love, affection and kindness in this boy's home — partly the cause of his misdemeanours.

(*f*) I, as well as three other girls in our club, — entering a competition for sewing.

(*g*) There — been at times a serious conflict of opinion on some of the issues we have debated.

(*h*) Improved transport, in the form of motor-cycles, cars and aeroplanes, — helped us to travel more quickly.

(*i*) You, together with all the boys and girls who took part in the escapade, — to report to me at 4 o'clock.

(*j*) This necklace together with these two rings — been in my possession for nearly twenty years.

2. Where necessary, correct the following sentences: (Some of the sentences are correct.)

(*a*) Yearly the traffic on British roads increase and the rate of accidents mount.

(*b*) The great ocean with its many mysteries fascinate both young and old.

(*c*) The author and critic have passed away.

(*d*) There was still twenty sheep to be transported to the station.

(*e*) Bread and butter are what I usually have for breakfast.

(*f*) Not only I, but also my parents are disgusted at your behaviour.

(*g*) The high standard set years ago by those who made our radio and television sets have been maintained right up to the present time.

(*h*) The fifth and final act of *Macbeth* contain the sleep-walking scene.

(*i*) The new Director of Education and Secretary to the Education Committee have made a good impression on the Council.

(*j*) I have just heard that one of the big hotels here is engaging six more waiters.

(*k*) A black and a white jersey is missing.

(*l*) Our list of forthcoming books together with full details of their contents are now for sale.

(*m*) A knowledge of at least two sciences are required to pass the examination.

(*n*) The iron and steel industry is affected.

(*o*) Information concerning new processes and products are now widely distributed.

(*p*) The gay life aboard some of our large passenger liners appeals to many tourists.

4. *Either, neither, each, none, every*

(*a*) *Either*, *neither*, and *each* used as pronouns take a singular verb:

Either of these methods *is* satisfactory.

Neither of the workmen *has* any reason for complaint.
Each of my sisters *has* collected £1 for the orphanage.

(*b*) *None* may be followed either by a singular verb or by a plural verb according to the sense:

Of all the days in the week none *is* more pleasant to me than Sunday.

Here *none* is equivalent to "not one" (of the days).

None of the people who took part in the race *were* willing to abide by the decision of the referee.

Here *none* is equivalent to "not any" (of the people).

(*c*) *Either*, *neither*, *each*, *every*. When the subject is one of these four words followed by a noun (i.e. when they are used as adjectives), the verb is in the singular:

Either prospectus *satisfies* me.
Neither programme *gives* me much pleasure.
Each boy *is* responsible for himself alone.
Every horse in the stable *has* been shod.

Note that a singular verb is used in the following sentence:

Every boy and *every* girl *was* tested for physical fitness.

5. *Either . . . or, Neither . . . nor*

(*a*) When two singular subjects are joined by *either* . . . . *or* or by *neither* . . . . *nor*, the verb is in the singular. When there are two plural subjects, the verb is in the plural:

Either the baker or the milkman *is* knocking at the door.

Neither the manufacturers nor the wholesalers *have* explained the reason for the delay.

(*b*) When a singular subject is joined to a plural subject, put the plural subject second and the verb in the plural:

Either James or his two companions *are* responsible for the destruction of the plant.

(*c*) When the two subjects are not of the same person, the verb agrees in person and number with the second subject:

Either you (2nd person) or Mary (3rd person) *is* expected to help with the housework.

Neither John (3rd person) nor I (1st person) *am* prepared to make such a great sacrifice.

EXERCISE

Insert one of the following words in the blank spaces: *am*, *is*, *are*, *was*, *were*, *has*, *have*:

(*a*) Each of the main branches of the subject — useful to an engineer.

(*b*) I am sure that neither the house nor its contents — for sale.

(*c*) Every hill and every stream — clearly marked on the map.

(*d*) Each candidate — given an intelligence test.

(*e*) None of the guests — late for the ceremony.

(*f*) Either my brother or I — to weed the garden this morning.

(*g*) Neither soldiers nor sailors — allowed to enter this building.

(*h*) None of the books — been stamped.

(*i*) Neither of my children — a studious mind.

(*j*) Either you or your cousin — not speaking the truth.

6. Collective Nouns

A collective noun is the name given to a collection or group of persons or things: e.g. a *company* of actors; a *fleet* of ships; a *bunch* of grapes; a *set* of tools; a *pack* of wolves. A collective noun is followed by a singular or a plural verb according to the sense:

The committee *does* not hold itself responsible for the loss of any article.

The committee *were* unable to agree on the subject of slum clearance.

In the first sentence the committee is regarded as a body of persons, one undivided whole, and the verb (*does*) is in the singular. In the second sentence the persons of the group, the members of the committee, were divided in their opinions, and the verb (*were*) is in the plural.

Study the following examples:

The class *was* given a half holiday.

A football team *consists* of eleven men.

The whole flock of sheep *has* now been rounded up by the dogs.

The choir *were* all very pleased when the bishop praised them for their singing.

The mob *were* scattered by the police.

The crew of the sinking ship *are* now being taken aboard the lifeboat.

Compare the following sentences:

(i) The number of boys in this class *is* now 45.

(ii) A number of his friends *were* anxious for his safety.

To what does the *45* in (i) refer — to *number* or to *boys*? The answer is *number*; hence the verb (*is*) is in the singular. Who in (ii) were anxious for his safety — *a number* or *his friends*? The answer is *his friends*; hence the verb (*were*) is in the plural.

See page 61.

EXERCISE

Insert one of the following words in the blank spaces: *is, are, was, were, has, have:*

(*a*) The troop — advancing slowly in the direction of the beleaguered castle.

(*b*) A large number of similar expressions — in accordance with current usage.

(*c*) The gang of thieves — soon dispersed by the police.

(*d*) The congregation — asked to stand up.

(*e*) A herd of buffaloes — stampeding across the open ground.

(*f*) A sheaf of arrows — all you require to take with you this afternoon.

(*g*) The regiment — lived up to its reputation.

(*h*) The jury — absent for nearly three hours.

(*i*) The committee — ill at ease when they heard about the condition of some of the houses.

(*j*) The Council — much pleasure in offering you the appointment.

7. The Verb in an Adjective Clause

(*a*) The verb in an adjective clause must agree in number with the antecedent to the relative pronoun:

> One of the best *books* that *have* ever been written is undoubtedly *Lorna Doone*.

The antecedent to the relative pronoun *that* is *books* (plural), not *one* (singular); hence the plural verb *have*, not the singular *has*, is required.

> Neither of the *boys* who *were* questioned was able to give the correct answer.

The antecedent to the relative pronoun *who* is *boys* (plural); hence the plural verb *were* is required.

> This is the only *one* of the paintings in the exhibition that *is* not on sale to the public.

The antecedent to the relative pronoun *that* is *one* (only one painting is not on sale); hence the singular verb *is* is required.

(*b*) The verb in an adjective clause must also agree in person with the antecedent to the relative pronoun:

It is not *I* who *am* guilty of trespassing on your grounds. (1st person)

Is it *you* who *have* been chosen to captain our football team? (2nd person)

The people who *are* profiting by my invention should assist me. (3rd person)

EXERCISE

Insert one of the following words in the blank spaces: *am, is, are, was, were, has, have:*

(*a*) I was one of the lucky ones who — not captured by the enemy.

(*b*) It is not he who — a political refugee.

(*c*) I thought it one of the best plays that — ever been written.

(*d*) Do you still maintain that it is I who — spying on all your movements?

(*e*) I was the only one of the six cyclists in our heat that — able to qualify for entry into the finals.

(*f*) Seated in the front row is the reporter and photographer who — promised to advertise our new society.

(*g*) I am not one of those parents who — always worrying about their children.

(*h*) Every person in the hotels which — been condemned has been found alternative accommodation.

(*i*) My impression is that it is you who — causing most of the trouble.

(*j*) This is the block of flats that — being built by Messrs. Warner & Watson.

8. Plural Nouns and Singular Verbs

A number of nouns, though plural in form, take a singular verb.

(*a*) *News* is always treated as a singular noun:

Sad news *was* awaiting me when I arrived home this evening.

(*b*) The titles of books and the names of countries are always followed by a singular verb:

Gulliver's Travels by Dean Swift was published in 1726.

The United States of America *has* many sentimental ties with Britain.

(*c*) Each of the expressions in italics in the following sentences is regarded as a unit, a single quantity, and is therefore followed by the verb in the singular:

Fifteen pounds is more than the article is worth.

Three months is the maximum time we can allow you for this work.

Sixty miles an hour is above the average speed for such a vehicle.

(*d*) Some plural nouns take a singular or a plural verb according to the context:

Nearly three-quarters of my country *is* desert and unfit for habitation.

Nearly three-quarters of the people of my country *are* illiterate.

The emphasis in the first sentence is on *country* (singular); in the second, on *people* (plural).

EXERCISES

1. Insert one of the following words in the blank spaces: *is*, *are*, *was*, *were*, *has*, *have:*

(*a*) Mathematics — my best subject.

(*b*) Fifteen per cent. of the employees in our firm — been with us for more than ten years.

(*c*) About a quarter of the population in the country I have mentioned — on the poverty line.

(*d*) The news of these violent outbreaks, together with the comments on them in the Press, — made many people change their attitude.

(*e*) Lamb's *Tales from Shakespeare* — a favourite with children.

(*f*) About twenty pounds' worth of apples — rotting in the market.

(*g*) Two dozen eggs — all I require at present.

(*h*) The means of travelling from one village to another — improved during the past twenty years.

(*i*) Twenty miles a day for four successive days — too much for most of the ramblers.

(*j*) Alms — given to the two beggars who were standing outside the castle.

2. Where necessary, correct the following sentences: (Some of the sentences are correct.)

(*a*) The price of refrigerators have recently been reduced.

(*b*) This is probably one of the most difficult problems that has ever faced our scientists.

(*c*) The designer and manufacturer of the machine is a young man named Spendlow.

(*d*) He doesn't know that the object of the experiments we are carrying out in the laboratory are to discover whether the composition of these materials make them suitable for industry.

(*e*) Neither of my sons have very much initiative.

(*f*) It is not I who is responsible for the damaged chair.

(*g*) A blue overcoat as well as a mackintosh and a raincoat has been taken from the cloakroom.

(*h*) None of the six members of the administrative staff have been offered alternative employment.

(*i*) The House of Commons are not in session today.

(*j*) Two-thirds of the world is under-developed.

(*k*) Provided that neither your academic work nor your practical work suffer, we have no objection to your proposed scheme.

(*l*) Never before in Britain has there been so many accidents on the road.

(*m*) Either you or Mary are expected to run the errands.

(*n*) Not only you, but also Harold has a key to the front door.

(*o*) The audience was told to rise when the Duke entered the theatre.

(*p*) Here is the only one of the magazines I have examined that seem suitable for boys and girls in your age group.

VI

GRAMMAR

1. Nouns

(*a*) *Plurals*

Students sometimes make mistakes in forming the plurals of nouns.

EXERCISE

Write down the plurals of the following nouns:

housewife, valley, dynamo, thief, axis, gas, terminus, son-in-law, phenomenon, spoonful, sheaf, radius, photo, analysis, crocus, dwarf, daisy, handkerchief, memento, memorandum, motto, oasis, rhinoceros, salmon, commander-in-chief, soliloquy, reproof, apparatus, portmanteau, index.

(*b*) *Confusion between Nouns and Verbs*

Do not confuse such words as *practice* (noun), *practise* (verb); *bath* (noun), *bathe* (verb).

Constant *practice* will help you to overcome most of your difficulties.

My brother *practises* at the nets for at least an hour every Saturday.

An old Roman *bath* was unearthed recently.

One of my greatest joys is to *bathe* in the sea.

EXERCISE

Compose sentences, one sentence for each word, to show that you understand the grammatical difference between the words in each of the following pairs:

prophecy, prophesy; advice, advise; device, devise; breath, breathe; cloth, clothe; envelope, envelop; sheath, sheathe; wreath, wreathe.

(*c*) *Collective Nouns*

Take care that you use the correct name of the group (collective noun) with the people or animals or things that form the group: e.g. a *gang* of workmen; a *shoal* of fish; a *clump* of trees.

See page 53.

EXERCISE

Insert a collective noun in each of the blank spaces in the following expressions:

a — of musicians; a — of magistrates; a — of horsemen; a — of whales; a — of savages; a — of policemen; a — of grapes; a — of stars; a — of ships; a — of dancers; a — of directors; a — of soldiers; a — of newspapers; a — of arrows; a — of cattle; a — of insects; a — of geese; a — of sailors; a — of flowers; a — of aircraft.

2. Verbs

(*a*) *Past Tense and Past Participle*

Do not use the past participle when the grammar demands the past tense of the verb:

He done it without my permission. (Wrong)

This sentence can be corrected either by substituting *did* (the past tense of *do*) for *done*, or by using an auxiliary verb with the past participle *done*:

He *did* it without my permission. (Correct)
He *has done* it without my permission. (Correct)

Similarly:

He swum a mile. (Wrong)
He *swam* a mile. (Correct)
He *has swum* a mile. (Correct)

Do not confuse the past tense and the past participle of the following pairs of verbs: *lie* (intransitive), *lay* (transitive); *sit* (intransitive), *set* (transitive); *rise* (intransitive), *raise* (transitive); *fall* (intransitive), *fell* (transitive). An intransitive verb cannot take an object. The past tense and the past participle of these eight verbs are given below.

Present Tense	*Past Tense*	*Past Participle*
lie	lay	lain
lay	laid	laid
sit	sat	sat
set	set	set
rise	rose	risen
raise	raised	raised
fall	fell	fallen
fell	felled	felled

The following sentences illustrate the use of the present tense, past tense and past participle of (i) *lie*, (ii) *lay*:

(i) He *lies* on the damp grass and then complains that he is suffering from rheumatism.

She *lay* down to rest on the sofa.

The snow *has lain* on the mountains and in the valleys since we arrived here about a fortnight ago.

(ii) Pauline sometimes *lays* her exercise books on the kitchen table.

We *laid* our plans very carefully.

I am pleased with the way your workmen *have laid* the oilcloth.

EXERCISES

1. Write down the past tense and the past participle of the following verbs:

arise, bid, choose, drink, drive, drag, eat, forsake, rid, grin, ride, sink, stride, weave, fly, flee, drag, ring, wind, sow, sew, dry, hew, dream, pay, beseech, burst, lead, transfer, speed.

2. Rewrite the following sentences, using the correct form of the verb in brackets in the blank space:

(*a*) He was so tired after he had — (*fell*) the tree that he — (*sink*) into a chair.

(*b*) The seeds were — (*bear*) away by the wind and — (*strew*) all over the garden.

(*c*) He — (*spin*) round quickly and — (*lead*) the horse into the stable.

(*d*) After — (*bid*) a hurried farewell to their faithful servant, the two men — (*flee*) into the wilderness.

(*e*) The murderer was — (*hang*).

(*f*) Though many people — (*think*) that James had — (*choose*) the wrong trade, he — (*strive*) hard and eventually became a works manager.

(*g*) This manuscript has — (*lie*) here for about a century.

(*h*) Tom — (*grit*) his teeth when the doctor — (*wind*) the bandage round his injured leg.

(*i*) The ships were — (*lade*) with all kinds of merchandise.

(*j*) The blacksmith — (*shoe*) the horses.

(*b*) Shall *and* Will

The following table shows the use of *shall* and *will* as auxiliary verbs for forming the future tense:

	Singular	*Plural*
First person	I *shall* run	We *shall* run
Second person	Thou *wilt* run	You *will* run
Third person	He *will* run	They *will* run

If *thou wilt*, which is an obsolete form, is omitted, you will see that to express future time *shall* is used in the first person and *will* in the second and third persons:

I *shall* be glad to hear how you are progressing in your work.

A meeting *will* be held at six o'clock.

We *shall* let you know the results of our investigation.

I hope you *will* not be late for lunch.

I feel sure that they *will* arrive before the play starts.

If, however, we wish to express a command, a threat (or determination), a promise or an intention, *will* is used instead of *shall*, *shalt* instead of *wilt*, and *shall* instead of *will*:

I *will* go even if it pours. (Intention and determination)

We *will* despatch the goods immediately. (Intention and promise)

Thou *shalt* not steal. (Command)

If you continue to spend your money as you have done in the past, you *shall* not receive another penny from me. (Threat)

They *shall* rue the day when they first smuggled firearms into our territory. (Threat)

EXERCISE

Insert *shall* or *will* in each of the blank spaces in the following sentences:

(*a*) I — go immediately.

(*b*) If you — give me your address, I — send you the book today.

(*c*) As long as I am in control of the business, I am determined that Mr. Wardman — not be promoted.

(*d*) I — never forget the day I was made a school prefect.

(*e*) You—pay dearly for all the trouble you have caused me.

(*f*) I — not let you leave this room until you have apologised for your rudeness.

(*g*) — you promise to be punctual in future?

(*h*) I — say now what is in my mind.

(*i*) They — find very shortly that it does not pay to oppose my wishes.

(*j*) I am happy to hear that we — reach Teheran by noon.

(*k*) In view of his past record, I doubt whether he — be made a sheriff.

(*l*) — we have to book seats for the concert?

(c) *Sequence of Tenses*

(i) A present or future tense in the main clause can be followed by any tense in the subordinate clause according to the sense:

Main	*Subordinate*
He *writes* in this letter (Present)	that his train *is* scheduled to arrive at midnight. (Present)
,,	that he *had* a very pleasant holiday. (Past)
,,	that he *will* be one of the competitors. (Future)
I *shall* complete the work (Future)	that I *have* been set. (Present)
I *shall* complete all the additions (Future)	which he *asked* me to do. (Past)
I *shall* complete within a week the unfinished story (Future)	that he *will* be sending me to-morrow. (Future)

Be careful that *shall* in the main clause is not followed by *would* in the subordinate clause; or *should* in the main clause by *will* in the subordinate clause:

I *shall* be obliged if you *will* grant me an interview. (Correct)

I *should* be obliged if you *would* grant me an interview. (Correct)

(ii) A past tense in the main clause must be followed by a past tense in the subordinate clause:

I *was* unwell when our school sports *were* held.

The man *disappeared* after he *had* rescued a boy from drowning.

She *told* me that Pauline *would* be waiting for us.

There are two exceptions to this rule:

If the subordinate clause contains a statement which is generally regarded as true, the verb is in the present tense:

We *were* taught at school that there *are* 240 pence in £1.

He always *impressed* upon his employees that honesty *is* the best policy.

A subordinate clause introduced by *than* can be followed by any tense according to the sense:

He *ran* much better yesterday than he *does* (or *did*) today.

My father *was* more highly qualified than you *are* (or *will* ever be).

EXERCISE

Correct the following sentences:

(*a*) The ancients did not know that the earth was round.

(*b*) I would not attend the lecture even if I am paid for it.

(*c*) It is impossible to state without examination whether the child would be taken to hospital.

(*d*) Police were on the grounds to see that nothing goes wrong.

(*e*) I warned Ted that there may be danger from the strong currents.

(*f*) I regretted that I can't help him.

(*g*) He will consider it a personal favour if you would allow his son to leave at 3 p.m.

(*h*) I did not know of your intention to have given me such a large sum towards the building of the new college.

(*i*) Your brother tells me that you had been ill last Monday.

(*j*) All four boys decided to go to bed early, for they have planned to explore the quarry the following day.

(*k*) Such a scheme must be carefully studied before it may be recommended to the committee.

(*l*) I shall accede to your request if you would complete this form.

(*d*) *Present Participle and Gerund*

Both the present participle and the gerund end in *-ing*. The former, however, acts like an adjective; the latter, like a noun. A gerund can be preceded either by a possessive adjective (*my*, *our*, *their*, etc.) or by a noun in the possessive case, but never by a personal pronoun (*me*, *them*, *us*, etc.).

That was undoubtedly the cause of *our* losing the train.

Losing here performs the function of a noun and verb combined, not of an adjective and verb combined. It is the object of the preposition *of* and has as its object *the train*. It is therefore a gerund and is correctly preceded by the possessive adjective *our*. *Us* in place of *our* would be wrong in this sentence.

Compare a sentence such as the following:

I heard my brother Alfred practising on the violin.

Practising (="who was practising") is a present participle qualifying *Alfred*.

Study the following examples of the use of the gerund:

Pauline was upset when she heard of *Jack's leaving* for Gibraltar.

I can see very little chance of *your* ever *becoming* a skilled worker.

I do not object to my *brother's going* into the army.

We insisted on *their getting* into uniform immediately after the concert.

The captain told us to raise the net gently for fear of *its breaking.*

I hope you are not offended at *my telling* you of your mistake.

EXERCISE

Complete each of the following sentences by filling in the blank space with one of the two words in brackets:

(*a*) Excuse — interrupting you. (*me, my*)

(*b*) I have made arrangements for them to attend classes here instead of — having to travel to the next village. (*their, them*)

(*c*) I do not see the slightest prospect of — satisfying my employer. (*she, her*)

(*d*) The party started with my — playing on the guitar. (*sister, sister's*)

(*e*) We do not think that — coming this evening will interfere with your plans. (*them, their*)

(*f*) I do not like — prying into the affairs of other people. (*Doreen, Doreen's*)

(*g*) Such a long journey would result in — getting home later from work. (*his, him*)

(*h*) It is no use — thinking that you can deceive me. (*your, you*)

(*i*) My teacher was angry because of — shouting in the classroom. (*us, our*) (*j*) They glanced at the path and doubted whether there was any chance of — leading to the summit. (*its*, *it*)

(*e*) *Misrelated Participle*

Care must be taken that the participle (past or present) qualifies the word or words to which it is related in sense. Sentences such as the following are common:

After waiting in the queue for ten minutes, the bus arrived completely full. (Wrong)

After we had been waiting in the queue for ten minutes, the bus arrived completely full. (Correct)

Waiting in the first sentence qualifies *bus*. Did the bus wait in the queue for ten minutes?

Whilst travelling on the 10.15 train from London to Dover, an argument rose between two men in our compartment. (Wrong)

Whilst I was travelling . . . . (Correct)

Travelling in the first sentence qualifies *argument*. Was the argument travelling on the 10.15 train from London to Dover?

Realising that many boys were overtaking him, a great effort was made by our school captain to increase his speed. (Wrong)

Realising that many boys were overtaking him, our school captain made a great effort to increase his speed. (Correct)

Realising in the first sentence qualifies *a great effort* when it is really meant to qualify *our school captain*.

Compelled by his father to learn a trade he disliked, every opportunity was seized to avoid work. (Wrong)

As he was compelled by his father to learn a trade he disliked, he seized every opportunity to avoid work. (Correct)

It is not "every opportunity" which is compelled by his father to learn a trade he disliked.

EXERCISE

Correct the following sentences:

(*a*) Walking down the lane a rabbit darted in front of me.

(*b*) When swimming a sudden attack of cramp may cause a person to drown.

(*c*) Situated in a sheltered area of the Midlands, the winter has never been severe in that town.

(*d*) Going through the main door of this building, Mr. Lorry's room is the second on the left.

(*e*) After heating you should slowly temper the metal.

(*f*) Being fully guaranteed for six months, I feel it is your duty to correct this fault in my television set.

(*g*) Dressed in full marching kit, the perspiration poured down the faces of the soldiers after their long march.

(*h*) Having melted the butter flour was added until a thick paste was made.

(*i*) Whilst studying at a technical school, the elements of a trade should be taught.

(*j*) Plunging through the jungle a thought came to my mind.

(*k*) When making application for such a high position, some knowledge of the work is expected.

(*l*) On arriving at the house, my friend's mother was there to greet us.

(*f*) *Two Auxiliaries with One Main Verb*

A different form of the main verb is sometimes required when there are two auxiliaries in a sentence:

Many people have and are buying cars on the hire purchase system. (Wrong)

You would not write "have buying cars".

Many people have *bought* and are buying cars, etc.

Oil has and still is in great demand. (Wrong)

Oil has *been* and still is in great demand. (Correct)

(*g*) *Split Infinitive*

Do not split the infinitive unnecessarily by placing an adverb between the *to* and the verb:

We propose to immediately claim for the damage you have done. (Wrong)

We propose *to claim immediately*, etc. (Correct)

I want you to carefully and methodically revise all the notes I have dictated to you on *As You Like It*. (Wrong)

I want you *to revise carefully and methodically*, etc. (Correct)

The split infinitive can be justified if there is a danger of the sentence becoming clumsy or of the sense becoming obscure.

The following sentences are correct:

I have made up my mind *to really enjoy myself* on our boating expedition today.

Those students who are keen *to fully understand* the mechanism of this intricate piece of machinery must pay attention to what I am going to say.

EXERCISE

Correct the following sentences:

(*a*) I have and always will enjoy the thrills of the game.

(*b*) I must ask you to particularly take note of Rule 15.

(*c*) Animals can and are used to give us pleasure.

(*d*) Man's development has and always will be dependent on the wheel.

(*e*) My father could but is not buying a television set because he considers it a time-waster.

(*f*) A good deal can and is learnt from a person's hobbies.

(*g*) A great change in our attitude to under-developed countries has and is taking place.

(*h*) The Federation is and will develop gradually.

(*i*) It is in your interests to clearly and distinctly enunciate every word you say.

(*j*) I never have and never will support this institution.

(*k*) She has played tennis in the past but is not now.

(*l*) The diagram shows that this substance can, has, and is curing the disease.

3. Adjectives

(*a*) *Comparative and Superlative*

The comparative degree is used when two persons or things are compared. The superlative is used when more than two persons or things are compared.

He is the *stronger* of the two boys. (Correct)
He is the strongest of the two boys. (Wrong)
He is the *strongest* boy in the class. (Correct)
She is the *elder* of the two sisters. (Correct)
She is the eldest of the two sisters. (Wrong)
She is the *eldest* of the three sisters. (Correct)

(*b*) Other *after a Positive or a Comparative*

When it is essential to the sense of the sentence, do not omit the word *other* after an adjective in the positive or the comparative degree:

John is as industrious as any *other* boy in his school. (Correct)

The sentence would be meaningless if *other* were omitted, because John would then be as industrious as John, since John is included in the school.

The *National Tribute* has a larger circulation than any *other* newspaper. (Correct)

This sentence would also be meaningless if *other* were omitted, because the *National Tribute*, being included in *any newspaper*, would have a larger circulation than itself.

(c) *Double Comparative*

The use of a double comparative is wrong:

My sister is more lovelier than yours. (Wrong)

Lovelier is the comparative of *lovely* and does not require the addition of *more*.

My sister is *lovelier* than yours. (Correct)
My sister is *more lovely* than yours. (Correct)

EXERCISES

1. Write down the comparative and the superlative degree of each of the following:

good, bad, cowardly, far, dry, grey, little, pleasant, old, many.

2. Correct the following sentences:

(*a*) Which is the harder to learn — French, German, or Italian?

(*b*) This machine is superior to every machine on the market at the present time.

(*c*) My text-book contains a more simpler method of solving the problem.

(*d*) John was the youngest of the two children.

(*e*) The Duke of Wellington was greater than any soldier of his time.

(*f*) You can have either a hard or a soft court for tennis, but the last is the most common.

(*g*) China has a larger population than any country in the world.

(*h*) This plumber is the most skilled of all the other plumbers in our workshops.

(*i*) He is as methodical in cutting the lawn as in every task he undertakes.

(*j*) Our class has been discussing which is the most popular—the cinema or the theatre.

(*d*) *Adjectives of One Degree Only*

Some adjectives, such as the following, can be used only in the positive degree and not in the comparative or the superlative:

round, dumb, square, essential, unique, blind.

It is most essential that we should arrive before noon. (Wrong)

Omit *most.*

This gem is more unique than yours. (Wrong)

Unique means "the only one of its kind"; hence *more unique* is absurd.

This gem is *unique.* (Correct)

(*e*) Due to

Do not begin a sentence with these words. *Due* (to) is an adjective and cannot be used adverbially for *owing* (to):

Due to a cold in the head, he was unable to think clearly. (Wrong)

Owing to a cold in the head, he was unable to think clearly. (Correct)

Due in the first sentence does not qualify *he*, but introduces an adverbial phrase of reason:

Because of a cold in the head, he was unable to think clearly.

Use *due* as the complement of the verb *to be*:

It was due to a cold in the head that he was unable to think clearly. (Correct)

Due to is used correctly in the following sentences:

The collapse of the bridge was said to be due to faulty workmanship.

Mary's success was mainly due to her perseverance.

This money is due to me.

My next book, due (=which is due) to be published in September, is expected to have a large sale.

(f) Agreement of Adjective and Noun

Demonstrative adjectives (*this*, *that*, *these*, *those*) agree in number with the nouns they qualify. A singular noun must not be preceded by a plural adjective:

These kind of books do not appeal to me. (Wrong)

Those kind of books do not appeal to me. (Wrong)

This kind (or *that*) of book does not appeal to me. (Correct)

These kinds (or *those*) of books do not appeal to me. (Correct)

EXERCISE

Correct the following sentences:

(*a*) Here is a most perfect example to illustrate what I have been saying.

(*b*) These sort of people annoy me very much indeed.

(*c*) Due to our long and tiring march to the foot of the

mountain, we considered it advisable to camp down for the night.

(*d*) This pen is more preferable to the one I have in school.

(*e*) These set of figures show that we have made a mistake in our calculations.

(*f*) Due to conflicting evidence, the prisoner was acquitted and set free.

(*g*) What is most obvious to me does not seem to be obvious to you.

(*h*) One of the most junior boys in our class is the captain of our cricket team.

(*i*) Our train was late, due to a collision on the line.

(*j*) She is the most intelligent of all her sisters.

4. Pronouns

(*a*) Who *and* Whom

Use *who* (nominative case) as the subject of a verb.

Use *whom* (objective case) as the object of a verb or after a preposition.

(i) The man *who* carried my bag from the station told me that he has four children.

Who relates to its antecedent *man* and is the subject in the clause *who carried my bag*.

(ii) The ladies *whom* you invited to the exhibition are staying at the Regal Hotel.

Whom relates to its antecedent *ladies* and is the object in the clause *whom you invited to the exhibition*.

(iii) From *whom* did you receive this letter?

The pronoun is in the objective case after the preposition *from*.

(iv) This is the boy whom I believe threw the stone. (Wrong)

This is the boy *who* I believe threw the stone. (Correct)

Omit *I believe*, or place these words in brackets, and you will see immediately that *who* is the subject in the clause *who threw the stone.*

Who is the correct form of the relative pronoun in the following sentences:

A friend is someone *who* you hope will always help you in time of trouble.

The two noisy young men *who* you said should not be admitted to the conference are protesting loudly to the stewards.

Captain Hardy inquired about Bob's brother *who*, he recollected, was in the army.

Whom is correct in the following sentences:

Please tell me to *whom* I am indebted for these flowers.

Whom did they accuse of foul play?

Let me know *whom* we can expect to be present at the meeting.

EXERCISE

Complete the following sentences by filling in the blank space with *who* or *whom*:

(*a*) The artist — we commissioned to paint the picture has met with a slight accident.

(*b*) In the distance I saw an older boy — I thought would come to my rescue.

(*c*) My friend John Parley — I had not seen for many years paid me a visit yesterday.

(*d*) I am not prepared to announce — has been elected chairman.

(*e*) My grandfather to — my thanks are due for many gifts is noted for his generosity.

(*f*) Talking to the Archbishop is the person —, from

what Mrs. Parsons has told me, must have played a leading part in designing this beautiful cathedral.

(*g*) By — have you been appointed to act as my deputy?

(*h*) The pilot — we were afraid was badly injured escaped with only a few bruises.

(*i*) — do you think will want to associate with you?

(*j*) He is not the clerk — the manager considers to be worthy of a special bonus.

(*b*) *Defining and Non-Defining Adjective Clauses*

Defining. My sister who was awarded the first prize in the needlework competition is training to become a nurse.

Non-Defining. My sister, who was awarded the first prize in the needlework competition, is training to become a nurse.

The inference from the first sentence is that the speaker has more than one sister, and that *one of them* was awarded the first prize, thereby distinguishing her from her other sister or sisters. A defining clause is not separated from its antecedent (*sister*) by commas.

The second sentence contains an example of a non-defining adjective clause. The speaker has *only one sister* and it was she who was awarded the first prize. The clause does not refer to a particular sister but gives us some additional information about the speaker's only sister. A non-defining clause is separated from its antecedent by commas.

The relative pronouns *who, whom, which* and *whose* can be used either in defining or in non-defining clauses. *That* as a relative pronoun can be used only in defining clauses.

The following examples illustrate what has been written above:

The book *which* (or *that*) you borrowed from the library should have been returned last Monday.

I cannot understand why our neighbour's dog, *which* has always been so friendly towards us, should suddenly attack our little girl.

The soldier *whom* (or *that*) we saw in the woods is reputed to be the best shot in his regiment.

The chief pilot of the gigantic air-liner, *whom* you spoke to when you visited the airfield, is retiring after many years' service.

The centre forward *who* (or *that*) boasted about his feats on the football field was taught a lesson when he played against our team.

I have just heard that Mr. Jones, *who* has been attending to our garden since we moved into the house, is emigrating to Australia.

This is the girl *whose* brother was awarded a gold medal for proficiency in mathematics.

She came to this country and married an Englishman, *whose* sudden death two years ago clouded her life.

EXERCISE

State whether the adjective clauses in the following sentences are defining or non-defining and add commas where necessary:

(*a*) The table which I bought at the sale has been placed in our kitchen.

(*b*) I want the three boys whose gym slippers are missing to report to me immediately.

(*c*) We are rewarded by the loyal service we receive from our staff which is a most valuable asset to the business.

(*d*) The Earl of Upton who will be 70 next Tuesday is making good progress after his recent operation.

(*e*) The parcel that was delivered at my house this morning arrived in a very bad condition.

(*f*) I disagree with your statement that there are only three or four people in the world who can write interesting stories.

(*g*) Our local butcher Mr. Fenner whose goods are generally of very high quality has opened another shop in a neighbouring village.

(*h*) The comedian has received hundreds of messages of sympathy from members of the public whom he has never seen but who know him from hearing his voice "on the air".

(*i*) In his younger days he had been an accompanist which was perhaps why he listened so intently to the man at the piano.

(*j*) One of the foreign diplomats at the reception was M. Paul Steret whom I knew from the Far East and for whom I have the greatest admiration and respect.

(*k*) At the top of the flight of stairs two apprentices were attending to the engine which that morning did not happen to be running.

(*l*) In an argument you can always get the better of an opponent who depends upon rudeness rather than upon reasoning.

(c) *Case of Personal Pronouns*

(i) Me and my brother grew up to be healthy boys. (Wrong)

My brother and *I* grew up to be healthy boys. (Correct)

You would not write "Me grew up to be a healthy boy". A pronoun in the nominative case (the same case as *brother*) must be used to form part of the subject of the sentence.

(ii) Two newspaper representatives interviewed my friend and I. (Wrong)

Two newspaper representatives interviewed my friend and *me*. (Correct)

You would not write "Two newspaper representatives interviewed I." The transitive verb *interviewed* requires a pronoun in the objective case (the same case as *friend*).

(iii) May John and me go to the cinema? (Wrong)
May John and *I* go to the cinema? (Correct)

The two sentences before they were combined were:

May *John* go to the cinema?
May *I* go to the cinema?

(iv) Let Jack and I see whether we can repair this bicycle. (Wrong)

Let Jack and *me* see whether we can repair this bicycle. (Correct)

The two sentences before they were combined were:

Let *Jack* see whether he can repair this bicycle.
Let *me* see whether I can repair this bicycle.

The transitive verb *let* requires a pronoun in the objective case.

(v) He is stronger than me. (Wrong)
He is as strong as me. (Wrong)
He is stronger than *I*. (Correct)
He is as strong as *I*. (Correct)

The sentences in full would be:

He is stronger than *I* (am strong).
He is as strong as *I* (am strong).

Than and *as* are conjunctions, not prepositions.

Whether the nominative or the objective case is used is sometimes dependent upon the meaning of the sentence:

He sees you more than *I* (see you).
He sees you more than (he sees) *me*.

In the first sentence, *I* is the subject of the verb *see* understood; in the second, *me* is the object of the verb *sees* understood.

(vi) It was him who ran away with my cricket ball. (Wrong)

It was *he* who ran away with my cricket ball. (Correct)

The verb "to be" has the same case after it as before it. *He*, like *It*, is in the nominative case. We have come to accept, however, such expressions as "It's me" and "That's him".

We understood it to be *him*, not *her*. (Correct)

It in *We understood it* is in the objective case after the transitive verb *understood*, and hence the objective forms *him* and *her* (not the nominative forms *he* and *she*) are required after *to be*.

(vii) The secret is between you and I. (Wrong)

The secret is between *you* and *me*. (Correct)

Prepositions are followed by personal pronouns in the objective case. *You* and *me* are both in the objective case after the preposition *between*.

Here are some further examples:

The Chancellor ought to do more for *us* farmers.

Nobody but *me* has ever seen this river.

My sister will not speak against *him* at the trial.

For, *but* and *against* are all used as prepositions in these sentences.

EXERCISE

Correct the following sentences:

(*a*) With the exception of my young brother and I, all the members of our family are married.

(*b*) His parents have been on holiday at the same time as us.

(*c*) It was me who telephoned for an ambulance.

(*d*) They think that all us teenagers are of the same temperament.

(*e*) These books are for you and I to read.

(*f*) No women but we have ever explored this dense jungle.

(*g*) All of them are younger than me.

(*h*) May John and me play until it is dark?

(*i*) Let you and I divide this cake between us.

(*j*) You are to blame, not me.

(*k*) Me and my sister attend the same school.

(*l*) Alfred was surprised that it should be him of all people who should discover the missing gem.

(*m*) My sister is not as lively as her.

(*n*) She can jump higher than him or me.

(*o*) After lunch my uncle took my cousin and I for a drive.

(*p*) Did you say that us and the rest of the boys in our club will be able to tour the Lake District?

(*d*) *Reflexive Pronouns*

A reflexive pronoun (one ending in *self* or *selves*) cannot be used as the subject of a verb:

Ourselves take full responsibility for our actions. (Wrong)

We ourselves take full responsibility for our actions. (Correct)

Ourselves emphasises the subject *we*.

The photographer and myself reached the aerodrome at 11 o'clock. (Wrong)

The photographer and I reached the aerodrome at 11 o'clock. (Correct)

I myself see no objection to your proposal. (Correct)

Note. There are no such words as *hisself*, *themself*, *theirself*, and *theirselves*.

(e) *Omission of Pronouns*

Do not omit the demonstrative pronoun in sentences such as the following:

John has not been promoted because his discipline is not as good as the other members of the staff. (Wrong)

John has not been promoted because his discipline is not as good as *that* of the other members of the staff. (Correct)

That is a demonstrative pronoun and saves us from writing the more cumbersome "the discipline".

My views are different from your cousin. (Wrong)

My views are different from *those* (=the views) of your cousin. (Correct)

My views are different from your *cousin's* (views). (Correct)

EXERCISE

Correct the following sentences:

(*a*) Do you think that my work is as important as a draughtsman?

(*b*) Myself and two other apprentices were called to the office of our instructor.

(*c*) The houses in our street are more picturesque than in the main road.

(*d*) A book bound in leather is dearer than in cloth.

(*e*) The temperature will be similar to today.

(*f*) He hurt hisself whilst he was climbing the mountain.

(*g*) Thank you very much indeed for inviting me to accompany yourself and a friend on a touring holiday.

(*h*) The rate of absence of women is higher than men.

(*i*) Workers today have to travel further than a century ago.

(*j*) John wants a job that has better prospects than his father.

(*f*) *Inconsistency in Number*

Everyone should play *their* part in reducing the road accident rate. (Correct)

Everybody flung *their* hats in the air. (Correct)

The difficulty in the first sentence is that *Everyone* is singular and *their* plural. Strictly speaking, we should write "*his* or *her* part", but sentences such as these, with the two pronouns of different number, are now accepted as correct. Similarly, in the second sentence, *their hats* is preferable to the clumsy "*his* or *her* hat".

Note the following sentences, however, where there is no necessity to use pronouns of different number:

Every boy flung their caps into the air. (Wrong)

Every *boy* flung *his* cap into the air. (Correct)

All the *boys* flung *their* caps into the air. (Correct)

When a *girl* leaves school and starts work, *she* has more economic freedom. (Correct)

When *girls* leave school and start work, *they* have more economic freedom. (Correct)

An outdoor hobby is useful to a boy for they help to keep him healthy. (Wrong)

An outdoor hobby is useful to a boy for *it helps* to keep him healthy. (Correct)

The indefinite pronoun *one* is followed by *one's*:

One cannot be too careful in making their (*or* his *or* her) way through this crowded market. (Wrong)

One cannot be too careful in making *one's* way through this crowded market. (Correct)

EXERCISE

Copy out the sentences that are right and correct those that are wrong:

(*a*) Even if one does not own an animal, they can at least appreciate their services to mankind.

(*b*) A person is sometimes accused of a crime which they did not commit.

(*c*) The way you spend your leisure time is up to the person themselves.

(*d*) A compass is made of hard steel so that they will not bend or break when they are dropped.

(*e*) A good memory is an advantage to a librarian because he or she needs to remember the names of so many books.

(*f*) Everyone was enjoying themselves.

(*g*) Every diagram and every picture has been placed in their correct position on the wall.

(*h*) This map will enable anyone to find their direction if they are lost in our town.

(*i*) If you were to ask any girl in our club the name of our local M.P., they would not be able to tell you.

(*j*) One should not be so foolish as to betray their ignorance by speaking on a subject about which they know little.

5. Adverbs

(a) *Formation of Adverbs*

See that you spell the adverbs correctly when you form them from verbs, adjectives or nouns.

EXERCISE

Form adverbs from the following:

persuasion, instinct, problem, honour, dictator, true, valour, happy, necessary, merit, skill, incident, menace, decision, hot, gay, essence, notice, extraordinary, argument, mischief, public, succeed, ice, regret, impartial, agree, rebel, hoarse, child.

(*b*) *Confusion of Adjectives and Adverbs*

He talks French too quick for me to understand him. (Wrong)

He talks French too *quickly* for me to understand him. (Correct)

The adverb *quickly* is required in place of the adjective *quick* to modify the verb *talks*. It is not *he* that is *too quick*.

These articles can be made cheaper by machine than by hand. (Wrong)

These articles can be made *more cheaply* by machine than by hand. (Correct)

More cheaply governs *can be made* and does not qualify *These articles*.

The tendency is towards the dropping of the *-ly* in the adverb forms:

The sun shines *bright*.
She works *hard* from morning till night.
Hold *tight* to the rope which I am throwing down to you.

(*c*) Only, scarcely, hardly, also

(i) A change in the position of the adverb, especially of *only*, may affect the meaning of the sentence. *Only* may be used as an adjective or as an adverb:

Only my teacher said that Stella's knowledge of physics is fair.

My teacher *only* said, etc.

My teacher said that *only* Stella's knowledge, etc.

My teacher said that Stella's knowledge of physics is *only* fair.

In which of these four sentences in *only* used as an adjective, and in which as an adverb?

(ii) *Scarcely* and *hardly* are followed by *when*, not *than*:

She had *hardly* finished writing the letter *when* the telegram arrived. (Correct)

He had *scarcely* packed his trunk *when* the taxi drew up at the house to take him to the station. (Correct)

Compare:

No sooner had the tailor delivered the suit *than* Robert put it on for the reception.

Do not use a negative with *scarcely* or *hardly*:

I don't hardly recognise him. (Wrong)
I *hardly* recognise him. (Correct)

There was not scarcely a person to be seen in the streets. (Wrong)

Omit *not*.

(iii) *Also* is an adverb and must not be used as a conjunction in place of *and*:

The clouds dispersed very quickly, also the sun began to shine immediately we started our match. (Wrong)

Substitute *and* for *also*.

Sgt. Orgrave was the captain of our regimental football team when we beat the Shrewsbury Wanderers. Also he led us to victory against the Blackheath Foresters. (Wrong)

The second sentence should read:

He also led us to victory against the Blackheath Foresters.

(d) Double Negative

The use of two negatives, often for emphasis, is wrong:

He don't know nothing about it. (Wrong)
He *doesn't* know *anything* about it. (Correct)

He won't pay, neither now nor at any other time. (Wrong)

He won't pay, *either* now *or* at any other time. (Correct)

EXERCISE

Correct the following sentences:

(*a*) I can assure you that she did it accidental.

(*b*) Jack only repeated to us what he had been told by the foreman.

(*c*) He had hardly completed his inspection of the empty mansion than he heard the strange noise for a second time.

(*d*) Young people today develop a sense of responsibility just as quick, if not more quick, than those of my generation.

(*e*) I am most anxious to conceal from my opponent that I have bruised my leg, also that I do not feel as fit as I did yesterday.

(*f*) He won't give nothing away to charity.

(*g*) We had scarcely parked our car than it started to rain heavily.

(*h*) I only go skating, like my brother, when the weather is cold.

(*i*) The committee decided not to appoint him, neither for the position of chief clerk nor for that of assistant chief clerk.

(*j*) This plane seems to be moving slower and slower as it nears the ground.

(*k*) Our local technical college provides courses in carpentry and joinery, plumbing, brickwork, and painting and decorating. Also it has an excellent library from which students can borrow books on these subjects.

(*l*) He never did do a job satisfactory for me.

6. Prepositions

(*a*) *Prepositional Idiom*

English idiom demands that particular words should be followed by particular prepositions:

This morning's talks centred around East-West problems. (Wrong)

This morning's talks *centred on* East-West problems. (Correct)

My answer is different than yours. (Wrong)

My answer is *different from* yours. (Correct)

There are many words in the English language that can be followed by two or more different prepositions:

My sister *looked after* (=took care of) the business during my absence.

You are asked to *look into* (=investigate) this matter without delay.

We propose to *look* (=search) *for* the missing key.

Please *look through* (=examine carefully) these documents.

I *look to* (=rely upon) you in an emergency.

Consult your dictionary for the other prepositions that can follow *look*.

(*b*) *Omission of Prepositions*

Be careful that you do not omit one of the prepositions when two words in a sentence are not usually followed by the same preposition:

The Council does not hold itself responsible for *the loss of* or *damage to* any article.

The visitors were keenly *interested in* and highly *appreciative of* the performance by our club.

Do not omit the *of* in the first sentence or the *in* in the second.

EXERCISES

1. Fill in each blank space with the correct preposition:

(*a*) He appealed — the sentence.

(*b*) You are liable — the full amount of the duty.

(*c*) Do not be annoyed — me — changing my mind.

(*d*) All of us admire the way in which he triumphed — so many difficulties.

(*e*) He is false — and unpopular — his schoolfellows.

(*f*) The painting — this vase is superior — the painting on the vase — your possession.

(*g*) There never has been a conflict — France and ourselves on this subject.

(*h*) The money was divided — the three children.

(*i*) Spanish public opinion seems genuinely impressed — and grateful — the expressions of sympathy from abroad.

(*j*) The reckless driver was disqualified — driving for six months and warned — a repetition of the offence.

2. Write down one preposition that can follow each of the following words:

acquiesce, adequate, consequent, amenable, independent, remonstrate, conversant, demur, dissent, congratulate, deficient, relevant, instil, impervious, encroach, infuse, amalgamate, bolster, ineligible, irrespective, acquit, indifferent, deduce, addicted, exempt, destitute, intrude, detract, subsist, digress.

3. Compose sentences, one sentence for each expression, to show that you understand the difference in meaning between the expressions in each pair of the following:

live down, live for; reduce by, reduce to; admit to, admit of; confer with, confer on; prevail on, prevail against; attend to, attend on; take after, take to; set out, set to; act under, act for; keep to, keep off.

7. Conjunctions

(*a*) *Misuse of* like *and* so

(i) *Like* may be used as a noun, verb, adverb or adjective, but never as a conjunction:

Life on board ship was not like I expected it to be. (Wrong)

Life on board ship was not *as* I expected it to be. (Correct)

Don't think you can deceive me like you did my brother. (Wrong)

Substitute *as* for *like*. *Like* is wrong in these two sentences because it cannot be used as a conjunction to join two clauses.

(ii) *So* or *so as* must not be used in place of *so that* to introduce an adverbial clause of purpose:

The firm provided facilities for recreation so the employees could enjoy themselves during their leisure hours. (Wrong)

The firm provided facilities for recreation *so that* the employees could enjoy themselves during their leisure hours. (Correct)

I usually put a cover over my typewriter so as the dust will not get to it. (Wrong)

I usually put a cover over my typewriter *so that* the dust will not get to it. (Correct)

(*b*) *Omission of Conjunction*

Do not omit the conjunction in a sentence such as the following:

This picture is as good, if not better, than the one you bought yesterday. (Wrong)

This picture is as good *as*, if not better than, the one you bought yesterday. (Correct)

If the *as* were not inserted, the first sentence would read: "This picture is as good than, if not better, than the one you bought yesterday." Note the position of the commas in the sentence that is correct.

(*c*) *Position of Correlatives*

Correlatives are *either* . . . . *or*, *neither* . . . . *nor*, *not only* . . . . *but also*, *both* . . . . *and*, etc. Be careful to place these correlatives in the correct position in the sentence. It is usual for each correlative to be followed by the same part of speech or kind of phrase. *Neither* must be followed by *nor* and *either* by *or*.

He has neither shown by his work or by his conduct that he merits a special bonus. (Wrong)

He has shown *neither* by his work *nor* by his conduct that he merits a special bonus. (Correct)

Each of the two correlatives is followed by an adverbial phrase beginning with the same preposition *by*.

Not only is it your duty as a son to support your parents but also to respect them. (Wrong)

It is your duty as a son *not only* to support your parents *but also* to respect them. (Correct)

Each of the two correlatives is followed by a verb in the infinitive mood preceded by *to*.

Why are the first two of the following sentences wrong and the second two correct?

This machine can both be used for cleaning and pressing. (Wrong)

This machine can be used both for cleaning and pressing. (Wrong)

This machine can be used *both for* cleaning *and for* pressing. (Correct)

This machine can be used for *both* pressing *and* cleaning. (Correct)

EXERCISES

1. Correct the following sentences:

(*a*) The speaker said this so he should not be accused of boasting.

(*b*) He wrote so carefully that he neither lost marks for poor spelling or poor handwriting.

(*c*) You and your brother will be interviewed both at the same time.

(*d*) The boys studied hard so as they could get good jobs when they left school.

(*e*) The scene wasn't exactly like he imagined it.

(*f*) She has failed not only to quote correctly but she has also attributed the poem to Tennyson.

(*g*) My clerk either seems to have lost his way or to have met one of his many friends.

(*h*) We are not sure whether Frank is as old or older than Richard.

(*i*) The foreign ambassador was both noted for his charm of manner and wide knowledge of languages.

(*j*) You must either pass in French or in German to qualify for admission to Hurstleigh College.

(*k*) Play these notes like I explained to you yesterday.

(*l*) The investigation shows that not only were many mistakes due to ignorance but also to impatience and carelessness.

2. The following passages have been taken from Shakespeare. Explain why, according to modern usage, the words in italics are grammatically incorrect.

(*a*) Thou didst it *excellent*.

(*b*) This was the *most* unkindest cut of all.

(*c*) I protest, I take these wise men that crow so at these set *kind* of fools, no better than the fools' zanies.

(*d*) No man hath any quarrel *to* me.

(*e*) Thus the whirligig of time brings in *his* revenge.

(*f*) He does smile his face into more lines than *is* in the new map.

(*g*) Each substance of a grief hath twenty shadows
Which *shows* like grief itself.

(*h*) Antonio, I am married to a wife
Which is as dear to me as life itself.

(*i*) Then, Brutus, I have much *mistook* your passion.

(*j*) He's *scarce* awake; let him alone awhile.

(*k*) Nor I know *not*
Where I did lodge last night.

(*l*) The heaviness and guilt within my bosom
Takes off my manhood.

(*m*) And yet not so, since I am sure my love's
More richer than my tongue.

(*n*) You know my father hath no child but *I*.

(*o*) That is, not to bestow my *youngest* daughter
Before I have a husband for the elder.

(*p*) Yes, you have seen Cassio and *she* together.

(*q*) Therefore they thought it good you *hear* a play.

(*r*) Jove knows I love; but *who*?

(*s*) He *shall* think, by the letters that thou wilt drop, that they come from my niece.

(*t*) And yet no man like *he* doth grieve my heart.

VII

STYLE

1. Faulty Habits of Speech

Many errors in the writing of English, including errors in spelling, are due to faulty habits of speech:

He when out. (Wrong)

He *went* out. (Correct)

If he'd have told me about it, I could of helped him. (Wrong)

If he *had* told me about it, I could *have* helped him. (Correct)

EXERCISE

Correct the following sentences:

(*a*) We didn't ought to sit back and take our pleasures for granted.

(*b*) Your not going to tell me how to run this ship.

(*c*) I ain't got no book.

(*d*) He done it accidently.

(*e*) I at to close my eyes for a few moments.

(*f*) When I opened the draw, I found that my mischevious brother had disarranged the contents.

(*g*) On this machine everythink is done by electricity.

(*h*) I bought this pen extra cheap.

(*i*) The explorers left for the artic circle on 12th February.

(*j*) I fill sure that my brother's main object in taking private lessons is to improve his pronounciation.

(*k*) Every dav we read of accidents that need not of happened.

(*l*) The government are responsible for the maintainance of this highway.

2. Colloquialisms and Slang

There are many words and expressions (such as "shan't", "won't", "old boy", "under the weather", "pay through the nose") which are permissible in everyday speech, but which are regarded as undignified in serious writing. These words and expressions are called *colloquialisms*. If, however, you were asked to write a piece of dialogue, you would not use the language of formal written composition, but the words and expressions of spoken English. What you have to avoid, therefore, is misplaced colloquialisms, i.e. colloquialisms that are inapt in a particular set of circumstances. Colloquialisms, for example, would be out of place in an Act of Parliament, or in a letter of application for a job, or in a report on the condition of the machines in an engineering works. Less defensible still in ordinary English prose is the use of slang (such as "bloke", "fluke", "a smashing job", "to kid someone", "to kick the bucket").

EXERCISES

1. Rewrite the following sentences, keeping the same meaning but avoiding the use of slang and colloquialisms:

(*a*) Most children are fed up after a holiday of six weeks.

(*b*) I nearly had a fit when I was told that my so-called friend had rounded on me to the manager.

(*c*) We met an awful lot of nice people at the party.

(*d*) The winner will receive a most fabulous prize.

(*e*) Harold got the wind up when he saw my father coming but he promised not to split on me.

(*f*) Jack's job is an absolute wash-out compared with the cushy one that I've got.

(*g*) That artful bounder has somehow managed to bamboozle us.

(*h*) My sister likes pulling my leg.

(*i*) I came to the conclusion that he was off his chump.

(*j*) The bandit stepped on the gas and made his getaway before the cops could get at him.

(*k*) When my boss invited me out to lunch, we had a scrumptious meal at a posh restaurant.

(*l*) I had so much difficulty in getting him down to brass tacks that he really got my goat.

2. The following passages have been spoken by uneducated persons. Rewrite the passages in good English prose, paying special attention to the structure of sentences, grammar, spelling and punctuation.

(*a*) They was all in a better temper when they woke up in the morning, and while Sam was washing they talked about wot they was to do with the dog.

"We can't lead 'im about all day," says Ginger; and if we let 'im off the string he'll go off 'ome."

"He don't know where his 'ome is," ses Sam, very severe; "but he might run away, and then the pore thing might be starved or else ill-treated. I 'ave 'eard o' boys tying tin cans to their tails."

"I've done it myself," ses Ginger, nodding.

"Consequently it's our dooty to look arter 'im," ses Sam.

W. W. Jacobs, *Night Watches*

(*b*) "And 'ow long, might I ask, 'as Miss Matfield been in this office, doin' 'er typewriting? 'Ow long? Two munce? All right — three munce. An 'ow long 'ave I been cleaning for Twiggs and Dersinghams, coming 'ere ev'ry morning, week in an' week out to clean this office? Yer don't know. No, yer don't know, and yer Miss Matfield doesn't know. Well I'll tell yer. I've been cleaning for Twiggs and Dersinghams for seven years, I 'ave."

J. B. Priestley, *Angel Pavement*

(*c*) "I dursn't, guv'nor. I dursn't let you go. Them I work for would cut my throat as soon as look at me. Besides, it ain't no good. If I was to go off and leave you there'd be plenty more in this 'ouse as would do the job. You're up against it, guv'nor. But take a sensible view and come with me. They don't mean you no real 'arm. I'll take my Bible oath on it. Only to keep you quiet for a bit, for you've put it across one of their games. They won't do you no 'urt if you speak 'em fair."

John Buchan, *The Power House*

(*d*) "Listen, Jim," he said. "We bin pals ain't we? You an' me — we bin through all this business together. We ain't done nuffink wrong. We ain't crooked or rotten or anyfink. We ain't deserted or got scared in a scrap an' run a't on our pals. We don't belong in this dump. An' if you're goin' ter take a chance on gettin' a't, well I aim ter come wiv yer."

Hammond Innes, *Maddon's Rock*

(*e*) "The reason I gets on so well poaching is because I'm always at work out in the fields, except when I goes with the van. I watches everything as goes on, and marks the hares' tracks and the rabbit buries, and the double mounds and little copses as the pheasants wanders off to in the autumn. I keeps a good look out after the keeper and his men, and sees their dodges — which way they walks, and how they comes back sudden and unexpected on purpose. There's mostly one about with his eyes on me —

when they sees me working on a farm they puts a man special to look after me. I never does nothing close round where I'm at work, so he waits about a main bit for nothing."

Richard Jefferies, *The Amateur Poacher*

(*f*) "What I want, you know," said Mr. Tulliver — "what I want is to give Tom a good eddication — an eddication as'll be a bread to him. That was what I was thinking of when I gave notice for him to leave th'academy at Ladyday. I mean to put him to a downright good school at Midsummer. The two years at th'academy 'ud ha' done well enough, if I'd meant to make a miller and a farmer of him; for he's had a fine sight more schoolin' nor I ever got: all the learnin' *my* father ever paid for was a bit o' birch at one end and the alphabet at th'other. But I should like Tom to be a bit of a schollard, so as he might be up to the tricks o' these fellows as talk fine and write with a flourish. It 'ud be a help to me wi' these law-suits and arbitrations and things. I wouldn't make a downright lawyer o' the lad — I should be sorry for him to be a raskill — but a sort o' engineer, or a surveyor, or an auctioneer and vallyer, like Riley, or one o' them smartish businesses as are all profits and no outlay, only for a big watch-chain and a high stool."

George Eliot, *The Mill on the Floss*

3. Clichés

A cliché is the term applied to a stale, hackneyed expression that has lost its sparkle because of constant use. These ready-made expressions are great time-savers to those who write without thought and are unconcerned about the drug-like effect which their words have upon the reader. Such fixed expressions should be avoided. Examples of clichés are: "the fragrant weed"; "the Swan of Avon"; "a hive of industry"; "a kindred spirit"; "to jump from the frying-pan into the fire"; "to leave no stone unturned".

EXERCISES

1. Write down the meaning of the following expressions:

to stick to one's guns; to add insult to injury; to fall on deaf ears; to have a finger in every pie; to hold no brief for; to hit below the belt; to keep the pot boiling; to let the grass grow under one's feet; to make one's mouth water; to make on the swings what one loses on the roundabouts; to bury the hatchet; to burn the candle at both ends; to make bricks without straw; to give a person a wide berth; to beat about the bush; to lead a cat and dog life; to keep the ball rolling; to build castles in the air; to have an axe to grind; to buy a pig in a poke.

a storm in a tea-cup; straight from the horse's mouth; a chip off the old block; at the eleventh hour; crocodile tears; a fish out of water; an admirable Crichton; a white elephant; Dutch courage; a feather in one's cap; a good Samaritan; a wild-goose chase; a close shave; a skeleton in the cupboard; a nine days' wonder; the black sheep of the family; a wet blanket; a Job's comforter; a hard nut to crack; the thin end of the wedge.

2. Write down one word for each of the following:

pharmaceutical chemist; the altar of Hymen; in durance vile; the senior service; the nasal organ; the green-eyed monster; a disciple of Bacchus; the king of beasts; the fragrant weed; the gentle art of Izaak Walton; the queen of the night; the sacred edifice; the glorious lamp of day; an ocean greyhound; the staff of life; the sport of kings; the weaker sex; the great unwashed; tonsorial artist; the lower extremities.

3. Substitute the name of a person or place or country for each of the following:

the great lexicographer; the modern Babylon; the Queen of the Adriatic; the Knight of the Rueful Countenance; the Eternal City; the Iron Duke; the Garden of England; the Lady of the Lamp; the Wizard of the North; the Land of the Rising Sun; the George Cross Island; the Celestial Empire; the Father of English Poetry; the Emerald Isle; the Grand Old Man (G.O.M.); the Light of Asia; the battle-field of Europe; the Athens of the North; the Father of Lies; the Warrior Queen.

4. Rewrite the following sentences, keeping the same meaning but avoiding the use of the expressions in italics:

(*a*) The Home Secretary *has the matter well in hand.*
(*b*) *The sublime author of "Paradise Lost"* was born in 1608.
(*c*) They were *both tarred with the same brush.*
(*d*) She could *twist him round her little finger.*
(*e*) *There is not enough room in here to swing a cat.*
(*f*) You could have *knocked me down with a feather* when I saw how *immaculately dressed* she was.
(*g*) It is *a crying shame* that she now has *to take pot-luck.*
(*h*) Those *who hide their light under a bushel* are nowadays *few and far between.*
(*i*) The circus clown *sobbed like a child* when he realised that he *had come to the end of his tether.*
(*j*) The bride's parents *explored every avenue* to make *the nuptial ceremony* a success.
(*k*) He *left no stone unturned* to please *his better half.*
(*l*) He *went so far as to say* that there would be *a general exodus* from the hall if the speaker did not *mind his P's and Q's.*

5. The following similes are outworn and have lost their vigour. Substitute a more vivid word or phrase for the word or phrase in brackets.

as green as (grass); as cool as (a cucumber); as dead as (a doornail); as dry as (a bone); as heavy as (lead); as mad as (a hatter); as obstinate as (a mule); as patient as (Job); as plain as (a pikestaff); as pleased as (punch); as poor as (a church mouse); as proud as (a peacock); as sharp as (a razor); as sick as (a dog); as slippery as (ice); as swift as (lightning); as timid as (a mouse); as good as (gold); as warm as (toast); as flat as (a pancake).

4. Commercial English

Avoid the use of business English. Commercial English lacks vitality and freshness, and is often verbose and sometimes meaningless. Here are three examples with the commercial jargon eliminated in the second of each pair of sentences:

We are in receipt of your esteemed favour of the 6th inst.

We have received your letter of 6th May (or the month in which the letter is written).

We have instituted the necessary enquiries . . . .

We are enquiring . . . .

We are wholly at a loss to account for the recent upward movement in prices.

We cannot account for the recent rise in prices.

EXERCISE

Rewrite the following sentences in normal English:

(*a*) Enclosed please find our latest booklet on the subject.

(*b*) We shall take a very early opportunity of acquainting you with our decision in the matter.

(*c*) We have duly noted the contents of your letter of the 7th ult.

(*d*) It will be our earnest endeavour to give you the utmost satisfaction.

(*e*) Further to my letter of the 6th inst., I beg to inform you that we cannot at the present time utilise your services.

(*f*) Pending the finalising of the arrangements for the sale of the premises, we are of the opinion that the present tenants should continue in residence.

(*g*) We have to advise you that we have now contacted Mr. John Goad, the manager of Messrs. Downes, Loudon & Co., Ltd., from whom you will doubtless hear in due course.

(*h*) We should like to assure you in closing that the order will be executed with the minimum amount of delay.

(*i*) We wish to acknowledge the receipt of your letter of the 28th inst. and thank you for same.

(j) We hope that your good selves will have lunch with the directors of our firm when you visit our works on the 2nd prox.

(*k*) Re your esteemed order of 25th July, I regret that, in view of the fact that there has been a strike at our works, we cannot ensure delivery until after 15th September.

(*l*) I beg to tender my services for your kind consideration as a junior clerk in your establishment.

5. The Same Word in Different Senses

Do not use the same word in different senses in the same sentence:

> Mr. Lauderson is *a man of means* who first came to our notice by *means* of an advertisement he inserted in a newspaper.
>
> Write "a wealthy man" for *a man of means*.
>
> My *host* complained to his wife about the *host* of waitresses she had engaged for the reception.

Write "large number" for the second use of *host*.

Sometimes, even when a word is repeated in the same sense, it is advisable to change one of the two words in the sentence. Do not write sentences that offend the ear.

I *know* that you *know* several languages.

The second *know* can easily be replaced by an expression of equivalent meaning:

I know that you *have a knowledge of* several languages.
I know that you *are acquainted with* several languages.

A sentence such as the following is not very pleasing to the ear:

On the *screen* is a *scene* so often *seen* in Western films.

EXERCISE

Improve each of the following sentences by writing a word or phrase of equivalent meaning for one of the two words in italics:

(*a*) Mass production has *done* away with a large number of skilled jobs that were formerly *done* by craftsmen.

(*b*) The witness *stated* that the house was in a very dirty *state*.

(*c*) The *sounds* coming from the attic during the night *sounded* strange to the old ladies in the boarding-house.

(*d*) He thought he would *set* a good example to the apprentices by *setting* to work immediately.

(*e*) When I dismounted from my bicycle, I was told that the service I was *going* to *go* to began at 11 o'clock.

(*f*) This small lathe is evidently of great *help* to you in *helping* to make the finished article more attractive.

(*g*) The main street is *quite quiet* now.

(*h*) I saw a sculptor *shaping* a mass of stone into the *shape* of a human being.

(*i*) I have no *regard* for people who *regard* themselves as superior to me.

(j) One of my first jobs was to deliver some documents to an office some *way away*.

(*k*) The dockers *take* this material to the waiting lorries and then it is *taken* by road to Birmingham.

(*l*) I will do everything in my *power* to protect you against the evil designs of such a *powerful* man.

6. Unnecessary Words and Expressions

Avoid the use of unnecessary words and expressions. Brevity is a great virtue in writing.

Study the following examples:

Your new discovery will, of course, revolutionise our present methods of making soap. (Wrong)

Omit *new* and *of course*. The idea of newness is included in *discovery*, which means "something that is found out for the first time". *Of course* serves no purpose in the sentence and is mere padding.

My job is to investigate into the time taken by you to arrive outside of this station. (Wrong)

Omit *into* and *of*. The preposition *into* is not required after the transitive verb *investigate*, and the preposition *of* after *outside* is an intruder.

The reason why I do not believe his statement is because I myself saw him remove the vase from the shelf with my own eyes. (Wrong)

I do not believe his statement because I myself saw him remove the vase from the shelf. (Correct)

The reason why and *is* are superfluous. One assumes, too, that the speaker saw with his own eyes, not with those of another person.

In my own opinion, I do not think that the sole monopoly for manufacturing this article should have been given to Messrs. Rice & Burroughs. (Wrong)

I do not think that the monopoly for manufacturing this article should have been given to Messrs. Rice & Burroughs. (Correct)

In my own opinion and *I think* are synonymous. *Sole* should be omitted because *monopoly* in the context means that Messrs. Rice & Burroughs have been given the *sole* right to manufacture the article.

EXERCISES

1. Show, by reference to the meaning of the word in italics in each of the following expressions, that the adjective or adverb preceding it is unnecessary:

a strange *phenomenon*; a fresh *beginner*; a new *innovation*; a free *gift*; a joint *partnership*; a final *conclusion*; a total *annihilation*; in unbroken *continuity*; the future *outlook*; strictly *impartial*; perfectly *identical*; continually *recurrent*.

2. Rewrite the following sentences correctly, by omitting the words and expressions that you consider to be unnecessary:

(*a*) All of these games must finish by 7 p.m. in the evening.

(*b*) You are absolutely right when you say that there is a speed limit on this road to which all drivers should respect.

(*c*) My work is as equally important as yours, but, however, I do admit that yours requires much more pensive thought.

(*d*) I shall have much pleasure in accepting your kind invitation to the dance on 14th March.

(*e*) As mutual co-operation seemed impossible between the two directors, one of them resigned from his position.

(*f*) Being as it was only 1.30 p.m. when he returned back from lunch, he seized the opportunity to read about the immigrants into this country from abroad who had come here from other countries.

(*g*) The veteran soldiers, all of whom had grown old in the army, surprised us by not using spectacles for the purpose of reading.

(*h*) Up until a few years ago, a refrigerator was not considered to be a definite and absolute necessity in every home.

(*i*) I am doubtful as to whether he will return back from work in time to help and give us aid in facing up to these problems.

(*j*) If Celia had have shown me the questions she had to do for homework, I could have explained to her that it was completely wrong to write an answer to the second question that exceeded more than 200 words.

7. The Arrangement of Words

(*a*) A change in the order of the words in a sentence may result in a change of meaning.

Note the difference in meaning between the sentences in the following pairs:

He alone was able to lift the heavy weight.
He was able to lift the heavy weight alone.

Harold said after supper that he would visit his friend Maurice.

Harold said that he would visit his friend Maurice after supper.

Steve Williams, who retired from the Merchant Navy six months ago, saw his old skipper walking along Oxford Street.

Steve Williams saw his old skipper, who retired from the Merchant Navy six months ago, walking along Oxford Street.

(*b*) Words, phrases and clauses should be placed as near as possible to the words to which they refer. Otherwise, the sentence may become distorted in meaning or even become nonsensical.

Study the following examples:

Soldiers must be careful what they say to their guards if captured. (Wrong)

Soldiers, if captured, must be careful what they say to their guards. (Correct)

The machine stood at the end of a long field, looking extremely clumsy for the pilot to handle. (Wrong)

The machine, looking extremely clumsy for the pilot to handle, stood at the end of a long field. (Correct)

Being bloodhounds, the boy's football was quickly produced and the dogs were allowed to sniff the ball. (Wrong)

The boy's football was quickly produced and the dogs, being bloodhounds, were allowed to sniff the ball. (Correct)

EXERCISE

Improve the arrangement of each of the following sentences:

(*a*) You cannot realise how happy I was when I read of the presentation made to you in the newspaper.

(*b*) This kind of hammer is used for demolition work, having a large head and a long handle.

(*c*) I correspond with a friend who lives in Nigeria every week.

(*d*) Everyone in our home helps with the clearing of the table after supper, including father.

(*e*) I have been reading about a river in our local newspaper that has been only partly explored.

(*f*) Tickets can be obtained from the treasurer, price 10s. each.

(*g*) The manager of the factory said that Mr Collins had ordered some expensive furniture to be sent to his private address by letter.

(*h*) In the early days, the settlers arrived in Southern Rhodesia in their ox wagons, having travelled all the way from S. Africa.

(*i*) It was reported that there was only one case of drunkenness by the magistrates in our town during the Christmas holidays.

(*j*) Hundreds of men, women and children had awaited for weeks the docking of the slave ship in dirty, insanitary cells.

(*k*) I saw a tennis racket for sale in the second-hand shop along the road weighing about 14 lbs.

(*l*) The boys in our street, except during the week-end, if they have sisters, do not help with the housework.

(*m*) *For the Term of his Natural Life* is an excellent book about convict life in Tasmania which I thoroughly enjoyed.

(*n*) This sum will be paid to the widow of the man who was killed by the order of the High Court.

8. Ambiguity and Obscurity

Lucidity is an essential quality of all good writing. The writer who does not make his meaning clear may be compared to a speaker who mumbles his words. Both persons have this in common: they cannot use English as an effective medium for the communication of ideas. All that they can hope for is to be partly understood. Both, too, may be guilty of ambiguity or obscurity. A sentence that can be interpreted in two or more different ways is said to be ambiguous. An obscure sentence is one from which it is difficult to gather the meaning. If you wish to avoid ambiguity and obscurity, you must be clear in your mind about your intended message and free yourself from muddled thinking. You must place yourself at the receiving end — in the position of your reader; what may be intelligible to you may be unclear to him. You must also aim at precision in your writing (an approximation to the meaning is not sufficient). Finally, you should read through very carefully everything you have written and test it for clarity of thought and accuracy of expression.

Here are some examples of ambiguity and obscurity:

> Not many husbands like to wash up, but there is no necessity to make them do so when you can put them in a machine that washes away the grease. (Wrong)

The girl who wrote this sentence had no intention of putting *them* (the husbands) in a washing-machine. Write "the dishes" for the second *them.*

> If a boy stays at school beyond the school-leaving age, he gains knowledge for passing examinations. (Wrong)

The main clause in this sentence is not a very good example of clear expression. The writer does not mean that the boy's reward for passing examinations is the acquisition of knowledge. Rewrite as follows:

> If a boy stays at school beyond the school-leaving age, he gains knowledge *which will help him to pass examinations.* (Correct)

> The buildings have been inspected by Mr. George Rushdale the sanitary inspector, who has promised to get rid of all the vermin, his two assistants, and an officer from the Housing Department. (Wrong)

The perpetration of this criminal act by the sanitary inspector can be prevented by writing:

The buildings have been inspected by Mr. George Rushdale the sanitary inspector, who has promised to get rid of all the vermin, and *by* his two assistants and an officer from the Housing Department. (Correct)

EXERCISES

1. Show that each of the following sentences can have two meanings:

(*a*) He believed every story of oppression by the Prime Minister of Arcadia.

(*b*) I promise to complete the form you sent me on Thursday.

(*c*) The maid told Mrs Jones that one of her dresses was missing.

(*d*) According to the regulations, you have to pass in English, a foreign language and mathematics or a science subject.

(*e*) You are now on the ground floor of the building which I spoke to you about on the telephone.

(*f*) Mr James told his eldest son that he would reward only those people who had befriended him in the past.

(*g*) The colonel disliked the prospect of a winter campaign as much as the general.

(*h*) I am not making a tour of the museum today because you have influenza.

(*i*) I prefer to study European history to English.

(*j*) Must I paint myself?

(*k*) Men like gardening more than women.

(*l*) His pride increased when he was able to obtain a high position for his only son in India.

2. Rewrite each of the following sentences, so that it has *one clear* meaning:

(*a*) For a protective finish creosote should be used, but even when dry the dog should be prevented from licking it.

(*b*) As only ten boys from our school can go to the circus, I propose to draw them out of a hat.

(*c*) Many people have mincing machines in their homes as well as in the butchers' shops.

(*d*) The engineman must once every week himself examine his two safety valves.

(*e*) A complimentary copy of your book should be sent to us on publication.

(*f*) Sir Joseph Whitworth after his death left a sum of money for scholarships.

(*g*) There is always the pleasure of rambling with one's dog admiring the beautiful scenery.

(*h*) Cows provide us with milk, and also goats to a small degree.

(*i*) When Mrs Tinsdale entered the club, she told the porter that she was one of the members' wives.

(*j*) The number of people in hospital now is two, not five hundred.

(*k*) I was keenly interested in your Italian adventure on television last night.

(*l*) My lawn-mower needs oiling badly.

(*m*) This tropical region is inhabited by white men and Africans of many different tribes.

(*n*) My friend caught a crab and we took it home in a pail of water which we had for our tea.

9. Pompous Language

Many students do not realise that what is simple and natural in language is more welcome to the reader than what is pompous and insincere.

The following sentence is a good example of exhibitionism:

> The traveller *proceeds* to the station, *purchases* a ticket and *endeavours* to find a compartment where he can *peruse*

without disturbance the *epistle* that was *despatched* to him by the manager of his firm.

Unfortunately for this student, and for others, we do not assess the value of a piece of writing by the length and weight of its words. *Goes*, *buys*, *tries*, *read*, *letter* and *sent* would have been more appropriate in the context than the corresponding words in italics. Do not hesitate to use the six words italicised in the sentence when they are in keeping with the subject matter, but do not try to impress the reader by inflated language.

In the following pairs of sentences the pompous writing in the first sentence is simplified in the second:

There is a dearth of information about the residents in this locality.

Little is known about the people living in this neighbourhood.

The commencement of the expedition was delayed owing to unfavourable climatic conditions.

The start of the expedition was delayed owing to bad weather.

In its initial stages the firemen experienced great difficulty in keeping the conflagration under control.

At first the firemen had great difficulty in keeping the fire under control.

EXERCISES

1. Write down a simpler word for each of the following words:

expedite, culpable, category, edifice, prevaricate, pedagogue, transmit, residence, approximately, expire, decapitate, succint, espionage, affluence, taciturn, colossal, indolent, adversary, benediction, demise, rapacious, taciturn, adulation, inundate.

2. Express the following sentences in simpler language:

(*a*) He retired early for the night as he was recuperating after a severe accident.

(*b*) A major consideration that must not be overlooked is that the scheme may not materialise.

(*c*) I have decided to terminate my association with your club.

(*d*) He was consigned to a penitentiary for appropriating Lady Portcaul's jewels.

(*e*) We located the missing document after a search extending over a period of an hour.

(*f*) It is not surprising that the family is in straitened circumstances, as Mr Toiler does not command a high remuneration for his work.

(*g*) You are the first person to donate a prize to perpetuate the memory of the deceased chairman of the governors.

(*h*) No person is permitted to perambulate the grounds of this mansion without prior consent from the owner.

(*i*) I could not converse with my teacher, as he was busily engaged in performing a scientific experiment of considerable importance.

(*j*) We propose to recompense Miss Jones for her indefatigable industry.

10. Mixed Metaphors

Take care not to mix the metaphors in a sentence.

> This great writer was at the peak of his fame in 1921, the key to which is to be found in the publication in that year of his *Trail of the Desert*. (Wrong)

Is it possible to have a *key* to a *peak*? The sentence can be corrected by using literal instead of metaphorical language from *the key* onwards:

This great writer was at the peak of his fame in 1921, because in that year his *Trail of the Desert* was published. (Correct)

The following sentence also contains a mixed metaphor, i.e. a sentence in which the images are confused:

Mr. Norton spoke about the wind of political change that was trampling underfoot all the old theories of native self-government. (Wrong)

An elephant, not the wind, tramples underfoot whatever is in its path. Substitute "blowing away" for *trampling underfoot.*

EXERCISES

1. Compose sentences (two for each word) to show the use of each of the following (i) in a literal sense, (ii) in a metaphorical sense:

pillar, storm, valley, wealth, paint, abyss, childhood, stream, collapse, pioneer, harvest, current, poison, road, torch, mirror, fountain, spark, veil, march.

2. Rewrite the following sentences correctly, avoiding particularly the use of mixed metaphors:

(*a*) One speaker claimed that the swelling tide of multiple stores was cutting the ground from under the feet of the small shopkeeper.

(*b*) As long as we have our backs to the wall, we must cloak our actions in a veil of secrecy.

(*c*) A storm of interruptions at the beginning of the meeting was nipped in the bud by the arrival of the police.

(*d*) Replying to his critics, the Minister pulled to pieces all the alleged pitfalls in the Government's proposed scheme to deal with the housing problem.

(*e*) The spy's hopes of a fair trial were shipwrecked by the mud of abuse that was hurled at him.

(*f*) Do not stab me in the back by letting the cat out of the bag, expecially when I am not present.

(*g*) Very few of us realise how quickly the sands of time roll onwards.

(*h*) One's vision is now being entangled by metal wires which stretch from pylon to pylon as far as the eye can see.

(*i*) The advancing chariot of civilisation has enervated the centuries-old influence of the African witch-doctors.

(*j*) A cloud of despair engulfed the countenance of the old lady when Sheila's avalanche of questions descended upon her.

3. Say whether you consider the word in italics is appropriate or inappropriate in each of the following expressions, and give a reason for your answer:

a *spark* of humour; a *lame* excuse; the *head* of a procession; the *eye* of a needle; the *foot* of a column; a *branch* of learning; a *run* on a bank; a *stony* heart; the *mouth* of a river; an *iron* constitution; the *teeth* of a saw; a *golden* wedding; a *dead* loss; a *ray* of hope; the *leg* of a chair; the *root* of a word; a *web* of lies; a *heated* discussion; a *light* heart; a *flight* of fancy.

4. Write down the objection to the word or expression in italics in each of the following sentences, and rewrite the sentences in an improved form:

(*a*) My belief is *he's downright crackers*.

(*b*) I must *acquaint you with the fact* that the man had been drinking heavily before the accident.

(*c*) I *beg to inform you* that we have now received the goods which you forwarded to us on 2nd April.

(*d*) All through the night they wandered in the woods with the mournful sighing of the wind *singing* in their ears.

(*e*) I'm not *frightfully* keen to have Rosaline Jones in our boat.

(*f*) The *final* completion of the work is scheduled for 3rd July.

(*g*) Our *culinary department* has every modern convenience.

(*h*) An American has *smashed* the world's record for the 1000 metres.

(*i*) These people are less passive than you think, especially when they are confronted by an enemy force; they attack *themselves*.

(*j*) It came as *a bolt from the blue* to me when I received £2 for being the first to solve the crossword puzzle.

(*k*) We must face *up to* the situation bravely.

(*l*) It seemed *strange* to me that he had been estranged from his parents for over a year.

VIII

100 MISCELLANEOUS SENTENCES FOR CORRECTION

1. A friend is a person to whom you are very fond of.

2. One speaker anticipated the not far-off day when we will be able to sit at home and see on our televisions what is happening in Australia at the same time.

3. The gaiety, together with the fun and laughter of New Year's Eve, are over and another year has begun.

4. To the boys in the school the holiday was looked forward to eagerly.

5. Entering the cave, the humidity immediately became noticeable by us.

6. I would have liked to have come with you to the museum to see the special exhibits of the seventeenth and eighteenth century.

7. Due to this countries rising population, we must produce either more food from our soil or import more food from abroad.

8. If he'd have spoken to me about it, I could of helped him with the maintenance of the machine.

9. Your not going to tell me that you having a bad finger kept you indoors.

10. I am not suggesting that less people today enjoy partaking in a game of football than a generation ago.

11. Between each of our school sessions every day, we have an interval of over an hour for lunch.

12. Neither of the two girls who are studying hard for the Trenton Scholarship like me to disturb them.

13. Machinery has in the past and is now in the present helping us with our entertainment.

14. It was already getting dark in the market so the shopkeepers were selling their goods at much lower prices so as to get rid of them quickly and then pack up their stalls.

15. Once more I will have to start like I started a few years ago.

16. Coal is also used in the making of gas, but it is used not so much as it used to be used about fifty years ago.

17. The money was distributed by John and myself between the twelve poor children in our village.

18. There is a much more friendlier atmosphere in our schools now than when my father was at school.

19. Nobody but we are responsible for the sad happenings on this day.

20. I have to regretfully decline your offer.

21. For at least a century up until the present time, the shops at Christmas all over the country, have been very busy indeed.

22. Neither the townsman nor the countryman appreciate their surroundings.

23. One must expect to meet some people which they dislike at work.

24. Irregardless of what my brother says, one has only one's self to blame for an accident on the road.

25. The reason why I have phoned you is because I have just heard that the boat will sail in the region of 4 p.m.

26. These essays have been written by a penetrating and a shrewd critic.

27. Quite a lot of the members in the Ladie's Section of our club are shorthand typists.

28. I shall be very glad indeed if you would send me the goods with the minimum amount of delay.

29. The woman told her son that she wanted some cakes fetching from the bakers.

30. Children should be made to realise the value of education. Especially at the present time when there is such keen competition for good apprenticeships.

31. Pauline asked her father whether "he would allow her to accompany us to the dance in the evening after supper?"

32. I prefer studying history than geography or French but my friend prefers the latter.

33. His remarks are totally unconnected and irrelevant to the subject.

34. A person of 18 years of age, who has only qualified in four subjects, does not qualify for a grant.

35. The adaption of the play for broadcasting was the product of the joint collaboration of Ralph Ambrose and Tony Richards.

36. "It's not alright, you must come down quicker when I call you."

37. The girls were discussing as to whether our deputy headmaster had left our school after such a short stay for domestic reasons.

38. Ordinary people like he and I must bear up bravely when we are unemployed.

39. Everyone, even complete strangers, were deeply grieved when the old general passed away.

40. My sister neither has the personality or the ability to become a barrister.

41. The man injured his finger when placing a piece of metal in the vice when looking elsewhere.

42. The letter I sent to the private address of my old Principle was returned to me by the Post Office as it had on it the wrong address.

43. I will write you within the course of the next few days giving you full particulars about your three months training.

44. When I visited Mrs. Smith, I found her ideas very different from Mrs. Jones on the subject.

45. Music is heard blaring out of these dance clubs and also the noise and laughter of people enjoying themselves.

46. A regular presenter of one sound broadcasting programme and a much-invited guest to another, Mr. Hine's radio dramas have been widely praised by the critics.

47. The French Government is in no mood for wage concessions to the miners whom as we all know have called a national strike for Friday and Saturday.

48. My friend knocked on the door, also at the same time the telephone rang.

49. I, as well as my parents, sister and brother, are emigrating to Australia.

50. Having lit the primus stove, the sausages were soon fried and polished off quickly by the three campers.

51. "We are reading in class," said Josephine, "Shakespear's Twelfth Night, which begins with the line If music be the food of love, play on."

52. The dance hall was a picturesque scene when it was bedecked with the many celebrities that littered the floor.

53. Being as it was Friday afternoon and seeing as there was nothing more to do, I went home early.

54. Mechanics don't interest me because it hasn't got even the slightest connection with my future career.

55. Will we have to pay for admittance to the pantomine this evening?

56. He had scarcely packed his bags than it started literally to rain cats and dogs.

57. One should not dedicate themselves to one particular past-time to the exclusion of all the others.

58. Generally, the time limit for these studies is limited and so the student has to cover the course in that limited time.

59. The rise in the figures for employment this week indicate that trade can improve, and has.

60. On account of the fact that the United States are

richer than any country in the world, the poorer countries have to rely mainly upon them to feed their starving people.

61. Is it you whose been banging at the door so loud?

62. Those sort of boys who are disinterested in everything but themselves get on my nerves.

63. We nearly split with laughter when he layed down on the floor and began to mimic some of our most notorious comedians.

64. It is of the most vital importance that we should concentrate our chiefest attention on the specimens on the ground floor.

65. Many people were lining up in the queue as it reached lunch time.

66. Each boy and each girl have now been given pens.

67. I have never met a person who is quicker or even as quick as John.

68. The investigating committee report that in the vast majority of cases it could only question a very small percentage of the housewives in each district.

69. The shrieks and laughter of the children floated across the water nearly blotting out the noise of the loud speakers.

70. We first of all collected our books and then we went downstairs where we found the coach waiting for us and then we boarded the coach and in ten minutes we reached our playing field.

71. Let us, you and I, disassociate ourselves from any connection with this satire.

72. His design is submitted to the owner who, together with a panel of experts, discuss it and then approve or amend it.

73. His friend should be a boy of his own age, somebody with which to share the pleasures of life.

74. With regard to your esteemed favour of the 5th inst., the receipt of which is hereby duly acknowledged, we are

obliged for your yesterday's enquiry and beg to hand you our catalogue of lace curtains as desired.

75. He is most inferior in intelligence to all the boys in his class.

76. Driving along the road no view of the countryside is available, as electrical installations prevent the motorist from having an uninterrupted view on either side of the road.

77. I am sorry to tell you that the manuscript, that I posted on to my cousin in Nigeria, has been lost in transit.

78. Instead of them having to attend evening classes, arrangements have been made for these boys to attend one day a week at the local technical college.

79. It is not true to say that Mr. Porter is in a state of financial stringency, or that since he has been domiciled here he has come home on several occasions in an inebriated state.

80. Not only has he made every attempt to, as I am sure you will agree, to write an interesting story but to illustrate it also with humorous drawings.

81. In a cold war one nation often uses propagation to deride the other.

82. None of the boys who was questioned were able to say which was the best of the two plays they had seen.

83. The mass of the people have profited from their experiences during the past few years, the lessons are being learnt, the simple truth that men cannot take more out of life than they are prepared to put into it is now universally accepted.

84. You had better make a good job of the nets as there are some large shoals on the other side of the reef, and I am sure you would not like to lose them.

85. He is an awfully nice fellow and has a smashing job, but is inclined to over-exaggerate every trivial incident.

86. He don't act any different at school than at home.

87. Something he'd ate must have been the cause of his discomforture.

88. We are delighted to hear that Joan and yourself have accepted the invitation from Cyril and myself to be present at our fifth wedding anniversary party.

89. One years or two years imprisonment at the most are what I think he will receive.

90. Our club recently gave a banquet at which Mr. Herbert Sterndale, M.P., was the guest of honour, pre-cooked, frozen and re-heated on the premises.

91. There must have been nearly three million unemployed at the height of the economical depression in this country.

92. It was not me or John who were selected to play the part of Falstaff.

93. "The old actor," said Paul, "was sat in his chair, reading aloud from Macaulay's Lays of Ancient Rome, which, if I remember right, consist of Horatius, The Battle of Lake Regillus, and several other poems."

94. In early times, and even in backward countries at the present time, the task of cutting and threshing the corn is a long and tedious business.

95. Having answered the questions what were put to him by members of the audience, the meeting ended with a vote of thanks to the lecturer.

96. I am of the opinion that Mr. Bekton who is passionately fond of dogs would rather pay the fine than have them destroyed.

97. If I was you, I wouldn't have waited for him so long if he promised to be at the station at 6 p.m.

98. What annoyed Tim was us both going to the pictures together without you even telling him we were going.

99. Take my better half, for example; tho' the largest proportion of her time is devoted to household matters, she still manages to do a little social work.

100. The only alternative left to you is to tell your parents that you do not want to offend them, but you really are

most anxious to go to sea & that you would like to enter a nautical college in order that you could train to join the Merchant Navy & not be compelled to go into the family business.

INDEX